PSYCHOLOGY OF EMOTIONS, MOTIVATIONS AND ACTIONS

HERMES, THE CHILD AND THE MOTHER: ARCHETYPES IN FEDERICO FELLINI'S DREAM-WORK

PSYCHOLOGY OF EMOTIONS, MOTIVATIONS AND ACTIONS

Additional books in this series can be found on Nova's website under the Series tab.

Additional E-books in this series can be found on Nova's website under the E-books tab.

PSYCHOLOGY OF EMOTIONS, MOTIVATIONS AND ACTIONS

HERMES, THE CHILD AND THE MOTHER: ARCHETYPES IN FEDERICO FELLINI'S DREAM-WORK

GABRIEL CAVAGLION

Nova Science Publishers, Inc.
New York

For permission to use material from this book please contact us:
Telephone 631-231-7269; Fax 631-231-8175
Web Site: http://www.novapublishers.com

Additional color graphics may be available in the e-book version of this book.

LIBRARY OF CONGRESS CATALOGING-IN-PUBLICATION DATA

Cavaglion, Gabriel.
Hermes, the child and the mother : archetypes in Federico Fellini's dream-work / Gabriel Cavaglion.
p. cm.
Includes bibliographical references and index.
ISBN 978-1-61761-338-8 (hardcover)
1. Fellini, Federico--Criticism and interpretation. 2. Archetype (Psychology) in motion pictures. 3. Characters and characteristics in motion pictures. 4. Motion pictures--Psychological aspects. 5. Jungian psychology. I. Title.
PN1998.3.F45C38 2011
791.43023'3092--dc22

2010033075

Published by Nova Science Publishers, Inc. † New York

CONTENTS

PREFACE

This book is written from both a psychological and artistic viewpoint in order to examine Fellini and his unorthodox yet extraordinary contribution to film. Fellini deals with another reality entirely, mocking social establishment as a whole. This book thus moves from pathos to logos, from Dionysian emotional and experiential chaos to Apollonian abstract and formal rationalism. (Imprint: Nova)

FOREWORD

I was born in a small northern city in Italy. My family was a middle class. My generation grew up in an affluent post-war age dominated by the Christian Democratic Party (*Democrazia Cristiana*). Nevertheless, the conservative Catholic school system of the 70s and 80s in which I and my age group were educated still maintained many of the facets of the fascist era in the curriculum or in the classroom discipline, despite the open, secular and democratic atmosphere. Many of Fellini's vignettes and sketches of his childhood classroom experiences are very familiar to me. In my family, strict, conservative educational ethics were transmitted mostly by my father, who was born in Italy two years after Fellini, in 1922. During his childhood and youth he absorbed and internalized many of these educational messages and transmitted them to us. My mother, who passed away at the age of 42, like Fellini's, was mainly the keeper of hearth and home.

As an adolescent I saw most of Fellini's movies, but I went to see them more out of conformism than for real personal enjoyment. I found his movies totally boring, with no plot or story, and completely devoid of the thrill factor that teenagers love. Sergio Leone's spaghetti westerns were more attractive, and delivered their (fairly predictable) message better. Moreover, influenced by the left-wing intellectual youth culture in vogue after the student protest and unrest of 1968, I found no explicit subversive message in Fellini's movies, unlike the mainstream neo-realistic films of the time. There were no clear slogans, no signification and no clear conclusion.

I had to wait at least thirty years to rediscover Fellini again and enjoy his creations. At that point I felt that my personal life did not have any clear direction, and that my personal plot was fairly confused. This is when I discovered that Fellini's veiled messages I had failed to perceive at the time are more than just subversive. Fellini deals with another reality entirely, mocking social establishment as a whole. This renewed encounter with Fellini's works prompted me to embark on this project.

One triggering event took place during a workshop on Jungian psychotherapy. The lecturer discussed the presence of universal archetypes condensed in a few scenes of Fellini's *Roma*. In these scenes a modern excavator named the "mole" discovers an ancient archeological find while digging to build the subway system in Rome. The lecturer dealt in a very explicit way with archetypes such as the anima and animus, the human quest for the Center (of the Self), the treasures of the unconscious inside Mother Earth, and the presence of the numinous in our past brought to light in our ephemeral present. What a revelation, in particular when, as an old established immigrant in Israel I had the opportunity to enjoy these scenes in my mother tongue!

About two years later, in 2008, the military conflict between Palestinian Gaza and Israel caused my workplace, the Academic College of Ashkelon to close for one month for security reasons. A large number of mortar shells landed in the city, one only a few meters from the dean's office. During this period of uncertainty and forced unemployment I decided to watch all of Fellini's movies again. Those hours were a refuge for me from the reality outside and a nostalgic escape into a world of fantasy and the climate of my youth in Italy. This process became a kind of self-discovery, a way to reconnect to my personal past and to decode personal and universal symbolic messages. It became an exercise in memory, a personal *Amarcord*, a linguistic challenge and a psychological inner journey, not only on the intellectual level. According to Jungian archetypal school, processes of artistic creativity, imagination, dreams and trance-like states have a powerful alchemical power to transform any *prima materia* like lead into gold. Going to a movie, watching, viewing and experiencing the "imaginal" might have the therapeutic power to change the public's states of mind within a modern *temenos*, the dark cinema hall. The eyes of the spectator, are detached from daily and alienating routine, and can be immersed in a new experience. The eyes become gold, transforming the inner psyche (Ravasi Bellocchio, 2004). At times, collective pain and human suffering, sometimes dissociated by apathy, numbness, and a frozen heart, leaden and petrified can be transformed into gold, and feel a profound human and spiritual experience. This was my personal case, while in days of war, in "*giorni di piombo*"- days of lead, during the Gaza conflict I found refuge into the University movie archive to reconnect to another reality, out of time and place. In some sense, Fellini was my personal therapist during those days, my guide and stimulating conversation partner of my pathos.

After great pain, a formal feeling comes—
The Nerves sit ceremonious, like Toombs—
The stiff Heart questions was it He, that bore,
And Yesterday, or Centuries before?
The Feet, mechanical, go round—
Of Ground, or Air, or Ought—
A Wooden way
Regardless grown,
A Quartz contentment, like a stone—
This is the Hour of Lead—
Remembered, if outlived,
As Freezing persons recollect the Snow—
First--Chill--then Stupor--then the letting go—

Emily Dickinson

This book thus moves from pathos to logos, from Dionysian emotional and experiential chaos to Apollonian abstract and formal rationalism.

I owe my work to my patients in my clinical practice, many Jungian mentors who escorted mc during my studies and training as a psychotherapist, and to Ashkelon Academic College, for its encouragement and funding of the language editing.

I dedicate this book to my beloved family, which for two years respected my need to undergo, sometimes in a form of solitary confinement, this personal inner journey.

Gabriel Cavaglion, Kfar Adumim, Israel
June, 2010

Chapter 1

FELLINI MEETS JUNG

JUNGIAN STUDIES AND FILMOGRAPHY

Both Jungian analytical studies, with a particular focus on archetypes, and cinematic exploration of Fellini's works have a huge academic following, but there is very little literature that combines the two. Experts in Jungian studies who have focused on archetypes and symbolism in films have neglected Fellini's heritage (see for example the collected papers in Hauke and Alister, 2005), whereas experts on Fellini's life (Kezich, 2006; Alpert, 1988), and filmography (Bondanella, 1992; selected papers in Bondanella and Degli-Espositi, 1993; selected papers in Burke and Waller, 2002; Ravasi Bellocchio, 2004), have only briefly examined the Jungian influence on Fellini and the enormous impact of symbolism and universal archetypes on his work. The notable exceptions are O'Leary (2002) and Stubbs (2006) who analyzed some of the archetypes present in Fellini's works, in particular the Anima and the Shadow.

The lack of interest in Fellini's work from a Jungian perspective may be due to a general trend in Western film analysis. First, as stressed by the Czech novelist and critic Milan Kundera, unlike many great artists who are only fully understood after their death, Fellini may well not be completely understood by public and critics because the director's private fantasy world is unwelcome in an era dominated by kitsch culture and mass media.

> Fellini's cinema aims at demystifying the very mass culture mesmerizing contemporary audiences, a critical operation in which the

> voice of culture is always less audible, as little by little man loses his faculty to think, to doubt, to ask questions, to slowly examine the meaning of things, to be surprised to be original. (Kundera quoted in Bondanella, 1992, p. xx)

Modern Western film study is dominated by three major semiotic approaches to film criticism: Freudian and Lacanian psychoanalysis, and the various Marxist (and leftist Feminist) approaches that in their various guises have set the agenda in the field or research for the last thirty years (Fredericksen, 2005, p. 21). Thus the neglect of the analysis of symbolism in film studies in general can explain why Federico Fellini, who was symbolic par excellence, has not attracted much attention, in particular by Jungian scholars. If there are films for which a symbolic attitude is appropriate, if not compelling, as in Fellini's, "then it follows that the notions of meaning used in semiotic approaches are too narrow and in need of augmentation" (Fredericksen, 2005, p. 21).

Film critics were however aware of the changes in Fellini's work that shifted mostly during the sixties from neo-realism to representation and to *sign*ification (Burke, 2002). But they rarely analyzed the deeper level characterized by a movement from signification to symbolization, or, as I will argue, they failed to examine the presence of the archetypal and the symbolic in his work through an analysis which is merely deeper, beyond signs. In fact, a vital symbol, according to C.G. Jung, is always a layer deeper than a mere sign. It is the best possible expression of an as yet unknown and incomprehensible fact that is mystical or transcendent and psychological in nature. But although a symbol functions or is interpreted as a sign, with its unique meaning, it remains devoid of inner energy.

> When symbol and metaphor are reduced to commonplace labels for what is known, they lose their original strangeness and fascination. They cease to connect us to that which is other than commonplace… and so fail to shock, to surprise, move and inspire us by evoking the ineluctable mystery of the world. (Yeoman, 1998, pp. 32-33)

The paucity of Jungian studies on Fellini may also be due to general neglect of the issue of filmography by the founder of the analytical school. In fact, Jung paid little attention to the cinema as a symbolic form. In one rare passage, nevertheless, Jung wrote that the cinema, like a detective story, enables us to experience all the excitement, passion and fantasies without danger which have to be repressed in a humanistic age. Even though he did not discuss the impact of films on the human psyche, throughout his works his approach to art in general can be applied to any study of "imaginal" filmography.

Jung stressed that the psychic products he called symbols receive a cultural and conscious elaboration; within art, religion, myth and folklore such elaboration often extends over long periods of time. They manifest spontaneously in dreams, artifacts and visions (like movies). They are not confined to any one cultural area or period of time, and they present a wide range of meanings (Fredericksen, 2005, pp. 24-25).

Jungian psychology, and in particular the "archetypal school", headed by James Hillman, focuses on mythology and the images of popular culture as reflections of the conscious and the unconscious; there are individual and collective psychological configurations that determine the color and tenor of a particular period or society (Yeoman, 1998, p. 28).

In an era dominated by materialism, where our unconscious processes, images and dreams are still only poorly understood and explored, the cinema can provide a means and a space to view unconscious material, and meet our psyche. Like classic Greek theater, cinema has the possibility of becoming a Greek Asclepian *temenos*, a sacred precinct (i.e. a sanctuary of modern culture), a place to encounter the unconscious, a place for inner changes and spiritual healing.

Mircea Eliade argued for a numinous attitude to art in general. Even when the celestial gods no longer dominate religious life, they all retain a preponderant place in the economy of the sacred. What is above, on high, continues to reveal the transcendent in every religious system. In religious life the sky remains ever-present by virtue of its symbolism. This celestial symbolism in turn infuses and supports a number of rites of ascent, climbing, initiation, royalty, and myths, arrows connecting earth with heaven, legends and magical flights (Eliade, 1987, p. 128). The cinema is one of the ways of eliciting this process, an artistic and collective "big dream".

As neo-Jungians have claimed, a variant of the active imagination is stimulated in the cinema that engages in dream imagery and other fantasies and can be integrated into our psyche. This special place enables the psyche to come alive, be experienced and commented upon. In other words, in the Jungian view, art, like the cinema, can be seen as a collective experience which involves the creativity of the author/director, and at the same time an individual response by the audience to a deep, shared experience. It represents a rebirth of the collective, with a greater value on the subjective point of view of the individual observer (Hauke and Alister, 2005, pp. 2-3).

Jung postulated that there is a deeper unconscious realm, which he initially termed "primordial images", then the "collective unconscious", and finally the "objective psyche". These various labels point to the fact that the unconscious at this level is not (only) constituted by personal repressions of the conscious ego; i.e. by something once known (as in Freudian theory), but by transpersonal factors that influence ego-consciousness itself. When psychic expressions such as dreams, fantasies and works of art are in touch with the objective psyche they have fairly universal characteristics: they can exert an extraordinary fascination upon consciousness, but for reasons that transcend strictly personal associations. When they occur, they do so spontaneously, outside the powers of the conscious will. In other words,

> ...they carry large amounts of energy and have an energizing effect. These several qualities of the symbol make our symbolic experiences numinous. And they indicate a psychic reality to which each person potentially has access, but which transcends the bounds of personal history (Federicksen, 2005, pp. 28-29).

Part of this energy can be related to the notion of *archetype*, the most fundamental concept in Jung's work. This refers to the deepest premises of psychic functioning that delineate how we perceive and relate to the world. An archetype can be defined as a psychosomatic concept, linking body and psyche, instinct and image. It is recognizable in overt behaviors, especially those that cluster around the basic and universal experiences of life such as birth, marriage, male/female, evil, transformation, motherhood, death and separation (Samuels et al. 2003, pp. 28-29).

Archetypes manifest as instincts and affects, as the primordial images and symbols in dreams and mythology, and in patterns of behavior and experience.

By post-Jungian scholars, in particular by those from the “archetypal school” the visual was revalued as much as the verbal. The ability of the imagination’s eye is to move through the literal to the metaphorical. The objective of therapy, according to James Hillman, is not to induce individuals to be more realistic, but to enable them to appreciate that imagination is reality, and that reality is imagination: that what seems most literally “real” is in fact an image with potentially profound metaphorically implications (Vannoy Adams, 1997).

FELLINI AND ARCHETYPES

Fellini's personal life and his work present strong archetypal influences, in particular when the boundaries dissolve between subject and object, past and present, reality and fantasy, adult man and child, feminine and masculine, director and actor, screen and audience. Federico Fellini is an object and a subject of his movies. In this process he engages in a direct dialogue within himself, as a director and an actor, and with his audience. He talks to us and in this way he forces us to talk to ourselves. As Risset commented,

> Choosing a program of Fellini's films demands consulting the images arranged in the library of one's memory, encompassing objects outside (the films) as well as internal resources (memories and dreams). Fellini images destroy, or at least lastingly blur the internal and the external realms. They, themselves, are part of existence, and constitute a hidden resource for the spectator, representing a depth of personal epiphanies. (1993, p. 64)

Although it is easier to identify clear archetypes in Fellini's symbolic movies after 1960, even in his first creations starting in 1950, the kernel of these patterns is present. Fellini's creativity and connection to primordial archetypes can serve to escape from reality, but also escape to a different reality, one that tends to be ignored or devalued in our day-to-day lives. They offer us an experience that is out of the ordinary, one that is uncommon in daily life; uncommon by virtue of the passions involved, the events witnessed and, importantly, uncommon because of the individuality of the character of the story (Hauke, 2005, p. 151).

Fellini was "archetypal" by his very nature, circular in a quest of a Center, mixing the symbolic metaphor, the uncanny, the unconscious and the primordial reality many years before he encountered the works of Jung and the personality of Jungian scholar Dr. E. Bernhard. These encounters gave further legitimization to what was already present in his life and work.

Fellini’s figures can be interpreted as anyone and everyone. They are not Olympian divinities, divas from Cinecittà, but rather ordinary people, our "gods" who live among us. In *Intervista* Fellini explains that "strange faces" can be found everywhere, as in the subway in Rome. He sought out real people with unusual bodies. For example, when looking for plump women who could play Brunelda in Kafka's *Amerika* (in his movie *Intervista*) Fellini filmed a sequence that parades ordinary women, who themselves declare they have “Fellinian faces”.

Writers such as Willeford have argued that culture draws various boundaries between classes of people, for example based on family occupations or casts, or ceremonials and rites. The cultural entity made up of all of these people often corresponds to a geographical area with a boundary that demarcates it from a no-man's-land, or from the area of others who do not belong to the group and are hence in one way or another not fully men. This boundary often corresponds to order versus chaos, beautiful and whole vs. ugly and less complete (Willeford, 1969, p. 132). Fellini speaks the language of everybody, fools included. He speaks all Italian accents and dialects. In this way he subverts culture, order and class boundaries by creating a chaotic Babel of languages and cultures related to a primordial, primitive or preverbal reality. Like children or certain schizophrenics, Fellini speaks his own pre-verbal glossolalia, his peculiar mixture of languages. He "speaks in tongues," i.e., says things understood neither by oneself nor by others. If one speaks in tongues, one's rational will is impotent; from this loss of power the presence of a superior power is inferred (Willeford, 1969, pp. 282-9).

Chaotic glossolalia is often associated with episodes of religious ecstasy or trance and was considered proof of divine grace. Early Christians actually believed the speaker in tongues was expressing himself in another language or languages not known to his conscious mind, through temporary possession by the divine spirit (Walker, 1983, p. 956-7). One of the best examples of glossolalia is found in *Orchestra rehearsal* where there is a mixture of accents and dialects from different regions of Italy. They are blended to apparently form a harmonious chorus, but in fact, their backgrounds, bickering and insults start from the beginning, resulting in a total loss of discipline and self-containment. The well-ordered orchestra becomes cacophony that has to be controlled and disciplined by the (German!) director. "At the beginning was chaos", is an axiomatic genesis in Fellini's works. And from chaos the artistic light and musical creation emerges.

Fellini always insisted on the fact that he did not invent or discover anything new. Thus his creations can be seen as inspired by primordial ideas or archetypal forces. As the journalist in the movie *E la nave va* exclaims: "everything has been already said and done".

Fellini associates himself with archetypal work in a very straightforward way. In one of his interviews, when discussing his “un-started business” namely *Viaggio di Mastorna*, a movie which was never produced, but was always *there*, in "his mind" and *in potentia* Fellini talks about movies as a reality that is "somewhere" before the director discovers it. He stressed that the artist does not invent a movie. Like a collective archetype, like Plato's *ideal forms*, he discovers it, as though it were already present in a primordial collective archive, or collective unconscious:

> I was always convinced that my movies were waiting for me fully made, the way railway stations are waiting for the train to arrive. Probably you have heard about that place, that city, the railway stations that are called that name; you have never been there, but the little town with its square, the church, the city hall already exist, who knows since when. But to know it, what it looks like, who lives there soon or later you have to go there ... then visit it with curiosity, wonder and the flow of unsuspected memories, and now, finally, you can talk about it, tell its story, its atmosphere, the feeling it elicits in you. (quoted in Secchiaroli, 2000, p. 21)

When Fellini was working, his mind soared "over hill and dale" to find something that was already *there*, waiting for him, a *big dream* representing a higher and truer reality delivered to humanity and altering the course of life. He was capable of connecting to the primordial unconscious, collective knowledge and human archetypes in a very natural way. He just attuned. As Umberto Eco wrote about Fellini,

> if reality is not there to be represented, the cinema, before narrating, must recreate it, or, at least stage an illusion of it...representing reality is a matter of producing something pre-filmic, belonging to the order of the material, of the physical, of the three-dimensional, before registering it (and yes, deforming it) through the shooting and editing process. (Eco, 1993, pp. 293-294)

Even his profession was portrayed by Fellini as a natural step in the course of his life, as an event which was bound to occur. In Jungian terms Fellini found it natural to connect his ego to the collective unconscious, to the Self, and to move easily along this axis. As Fellini stated in his *Book of Dreams* with regard to his insights into one of his dreams, all that we can do is to try to become aware that we are part of this unfathomable mystery that is created. We obey its unknowable law, its rhythms, its changes. We are a mystery among mysteries. (Fellini, 2008, p. 553-554)

Fellini assembled and represented universal archetypes and in many ways was "a mediator between the mysteries of nature and the mysteries of man" (Calvino, 1993, p. 29). As Bazin pointed out, events do not happen in Fellini's world; they befall its inhabitants, they occur as an effect of vertical gravity, and defy the laws of horizontal causality. For example Fellini said (in Gideon Bachman's movie *Ciao Federico!* 1969):

> I make films because I discovered when I was 30 that this was the most congenial way to work, to live. And so why not to make pictures?(sic) It is not a problem of professional work, but it is just my way to live, to come closer to fulfilling to my nature, is just to create images. There is no other reason.

Fellini was always eager to accept innovation, develop new ideas, and turn common sense upside down to achieve his goals:

> Things presented themselves in a very spontaneous way, and I found myself living them naturally, as though everything was already foreseen. In my life in general I have never had to decide or choose… I found my movies already made. I had to create them of course, but they were already defined … in a certain sense already realized. (quoted in Pettigrew, 1994, p. 32, my translation)

This passage reminds one of the core themes in Jungian psychology.

In Jung's undifferentiated form of the uniform world, the potential world outside of time, everything is interconnected, and there is no difference between psychological and physical facts, past present or future. At this magical, pre-oedipal level of the psyche, which is at odds with rational and causal explanations, certain things just happen to occur together. And psychological significance may be experienced syncrhronistically through meaningful coincidences (Salman, 1997, p. 54).

In other interviews Fellini said that his movies started taking shape from the moment he signed a contract with the producers. Fellini was perhaps referring to the archetypal, mythological ground of our experience, as well the infinite variety of that truth, and the power of the image, of the "imaginal" to evoke and perhaps invoke its enigmatic presence; namely: "image and imagination may be seen, as the agencies which enable us to create our worlds in the first place, and to recreate them continually in new and endless possibilities" (Yeoman, 1998, p. 31). Fellini revealed the inner consistency, coherence and integrity that made him a man of the cinema, or in Jungian terms, a person with a good sense of individuation and connection to the inner Center in his own Self,

> My work, making films, is a way of being, not only a form of expression. Living by making movies comes the closest for me to expressing my own identity. The center of my history is where I find myself in the center of my existence. (in Pettigrew, 1994, pp. 20-21, my translation)

In this book I will suggest that the archetypes of Hermes, the Child and the Mother, with their derivates, the trickster, the mage, the eternal child, the terrible mother etc. are part of a constellation that characterized Fellini's personality and work. These archetypes present a unique idiosyncratic constellation under the God Hermes, in that each force is formed, influenced and fertilized by the other. The influence of Hermes on Fellini' life or the Hermes characters in his dreams cannot be separated from his artistic creations. Similarly the archetype of Hermes cannot be dissociated from his childish, tricky and magic character. The Mother is related to the Child, and the obverse, the Eternal Child, emerges from the ambivalent and possessive devouring forces of the Great Mother.

The processes that take place within Fellini's psyche, in his archetypal constellations, are not examined here. Fellini is not posthumously invited to lie on the couch. Even the analysis of his dreams, as expressed in his *Book of Dreams*, should be taken with many precautions and humility (Gaillard, 2009; Ravasi Bellocchio, 2009).

In Jungian terminology, I do not deal with Fellini's "psychic ontogenesis" (Stevens, 2002). Rather, this book examines the visual content of his cinematic works and dreams as they relate to symbolism, and the main archetypes are examined solely as an expression of a collective narrative, the "phylogenesis of human culture". In other words, this book is more cultural than psychological, and starts from the premise that Fellini's thought follows a pattern that "was established long before man developed a reflective consciousness" (Jung 1983, p. 76). In Fellini's work, these archetypes can be seen as an unprocessed primordial kernel bound to unconscious, collective content and processes indicative of our universal archetypes.

Archetypes, like myths, are a rich source of psychological insight. They are a special unwritten literary genre, the creation not of one person but of the imagination and experience of an entire cultural epoch. Therefore, learning about Fellini can be seen as a discovery of ourselves.

FELLINI AND JUNG

It is no accident that Federico Fellini has been described as "the Italian director most influenced by Jungian thought" (Carotenuto, 2000, p. 119). He was attracted to Jung's writings because of his vision of life, and considered Jung: "a friend on a journey, an older brother, a wise man, a visionary scientist... [allowing] us to imagine, to dream, and when entering the obscure labyrinth of his being, you can almost feel his alert and protective presence" (quoted in Carotenuto, 2000, pp. 120-121, my translation).

As an "older brother", Jung provided Fellini with intellectual support for concepts and artistic attitudes and human archetypes he arrived at on his own and with an iconography that he could use in his movies, particularly those with dreams in them or with dreamlike qualities (Stubbs, 2006, p.38). In one of his interviews Fellini recognized having something in common with Jung:

> ... Jung has been a friend of journey, one of those providential meetings which have nourished and cultivated me. Bernhard initiated me to some fundamental texts by Jung... and I felt I was protected by him (Jung) and walking alongside him, in particular in a period of personal creative crisis. (Pettigrew, 1994, pp. 102)

The study of Jung and his meeting with Dr. Ernst Bernhard, a Jungian analyst who lived in Rome and was the founder of the Italian Analytical Society, gave him psychological security, legitimized and encouraged his interest in parapsychology and the paranormal as part of his personal and professional interest and attitudes. From 1960, at the age of forty, Fellini had significant informal meetings and probably (despite Fellini's denial) formal therapeutic encounters with Bernhard (Gaillard, 2009). At this stage, he became more attentive, aware and attuned to his dreams and at Bernhard's suggestion began to write down and illustrate them as an exercise in self-exploration, creativity and as a means of inner growth, in what became his posthumous *Book of Dreams* (Alpert, 1988, pp. 167-170; Kezich, 2006, p. 225). Gaillard reports that the presentation of his dreams gradually became more open, more disconcerting, more adventurous, and at the same time more introverted (2009, p. 22). Expressions of fears, doubts, and disorganized plots (aspects of the archetypal *shadow*) became more frequent during the years. From the early sixties his filmography moved into dreamlike surrealism, where vivid archetypes became more consistent. Filming itself became a sort of fervor with overwhelming emotional dreamlike connotations (Kezich, 2008,

p. 15): "in a way the director bids farewell to reality, taking the gesture of cutting the umbilical cord to the extreme… [entering] a broader, evanescent, and intangible dimension. From this point we can say that for Fellini, life is but a dream".

In this inner process of transformation Fellini became more attuned to his dreams with their powerful archetypes that started to influence his work "as a way to express the inexpressible" (Carotenuto, 2000, p.122, my translation). But as Fellini confessed, reporting dreams was a difficult task: "It is another code of expression which belongs to another dimension where ideas, reason, the intellectual are completely excluded. The expression is done by symbols. Then the symbol becomes the most completed mode of expression" (in Pettigrew, 1994, p. 80).

The influence of Jung on Fellini was more than just intellectual. During different periods, in particular between 1964 and1967, both Bernhard and Jung appeared in Fellini's dreams, with their own "doctrine" as benevolent physicians and philosophers (dreams dated January 1965). They appeared as professors, doctors, healers, wise old teachers, spiritual guides who deliver an important message or a gift to the dreamer. One example is a dream dated July 1966:

> Lunch with Jung in the little piazza in a small Ligurian or Swiss town. Jung is a very handsome old man: what physical and intellectual vigor emanates from his robust farmer's body, his gaze is clear, acute, benevolently ironic. We are eating spaghetti (Liliana's is there too) and we bite into one that's the same strand and crosses all the plates. (Fellini, 2008, p. 502)

This dream calls for some knowledge of Fellini's free association processes and the general context of this particular period of his life. Nevertheless Jung appears as a positive, wise old man, and there is a message of mutuality and reciprocal "feeding" of emotions and spirituality, with spaghetti as a personal nurturing journey into the intricacies of life.

The archetypal figure of Jung as the wise old man also appears in a dream dated October, 13, 1966: "I dream of Jung, he's just like he is in the photo, with a handsome face of an old magician/farmer".

Fellini had a similar attitude to Bernhard, seen as a wise man who can deliver an exotic gift. For example, in a dream dated January 2, 1967:

> For my birthday Bernhard has given me a model-sized packet of Asian cigarettes as a gift. The packaging is brightly colored, full of drawings and little figures, it looks like a pack of playing cards. I embrace B. on the cheeks and hold my hands around his head… I wanted to give him a gift in return…

Bernhard is also a good friend and their intimacy appears in a dream where he is invited to dream in his house "in his bed!" (November 20, 1963).

The fear of Bernhard's death, which actually occurred around the time of this dream, is compensated for by the immortal spiritual message he received from his teacher. In a dream dated May 5, 1965:

> Bernard is dead! … His head is bandaged, his teeth uncovered and this strikes me because it seems like he's been dead for a long time, nothing has putrefied, nothing's wet, everything's dry, dusty, incredibly old. The professor's spirit rises evanescent and extremely tall from the cadaver, shaking my hands with great strength as if to show me that the soul is immortal and stronger than anything…

Month later, Bernhard, in a dream dated February 14, 1966 (Fellini, 2008, p. 500), appears as the deliverer of a deep eternal spiritual message and as a spiritual guide in a period of Fellini's personal crisis. He says to Fellini: "I am a Guru. This is how you should try to portray me".

The appearance of Jung and his disciple Bernhard in Fellini's dreams coincides with a spiritual interest in the analytical school, but also with the need to find some relief from his personal midlife crisis, mostly characterized by insomnia, inner unrest, emptiness and depression. Fellini was aware of his inner crises as well as Jung was aware of his own. Fellini had read Jung's memoirs and knew about the professor's crises (Gaillard, 2009, p. 17). Both found comfort and personal expression through artistic creation, an exit or a way to self-realization of the unconscious. For example, Jung wrote in his memoirs:

> After the parting of the ways with Freud, a period of inner uncertainty began for me. It would be no exaggeration to call it a state of disorientation. I felt totally suspended in mid-air, for I had not yet found my footing… I avoided all theoretical points of view and simply helped the patients to understand the dream-images by themselves, without application of rules and theories. (1963, p. 165)

Elsewhere he writes:

> In order to seize hold of the fantasies, I frequently imagined a steep descent. I even made several attempts to get to the very bottom. The first time I reached, as it were, a depth of about a thousand feet; the next time I found myself at the edge of a cosmic abyss. It was like a voyage to the moon, or a descent into empty space. First came the image of a crater, and I had the feeling that I was in the land of the dead. The atmosphere was that of the other world. (Jung, 1963, p. 174)

But after reaching the bottom Jung was able to be reborn, by tapping into his own creativity (to use his term, his own *Gestaltung*)

> From the beginning I felt the Tower [a building he constructed close to his house, in Bollingen, following deep intuition and mystical insights] was in some way a place of maturation – a maternal womb or a maternal figure in which I could become what I was, what I am and will be. It gave me a feeling I were being reborn in stone…(there) I am in the midst of my true life, I am most deeply myself. (Jung, 1963, pp. 213-4)

During this period Jung learns how to cut and dress stone with only occasional professional help. He sets about building a second home composed of a thick-set tower. He calls it simply “Bollingen” and, for the remainder of his life, he retires there to seek quiet and renewal. He also takes up carving in stone, for therapeutic rather than artistic purposes.

Fellini's midlife, a period of crisis, which is well expressed by his autobiographical movie *8½*, and in his dreams, was also a period of personal revival in which a new flow of creativity started to be born, when his "Tower" in Rome's Cinecittà studios became the place of his true life. Through their experience with personal crises, both Jung and Fellini had a empathetic attitude toward the insane and lunatics. Fellini portrays Ivo’s hallucinations in *La voce della luna* as a “great gift”, and the moon tells him that he should stop complaining about not understanding these voices: “you make me angry you’re so lucky. You mustn’t understand! It would be terrible if you understood! And what would you do then? You must only listen to them, only hear those voices and hope that they never tire of calling you” (translated by Bondanella, 1992, p. 331).

Ivo, like Fellini, and Jung, used creativity as a solution to his disorientation and inner "madness". In Fellini's inner experience, the need for artistic order is clearly expressed in the following dream, dated January 10, 1967

> The insane asylum, devastated by faces, rendered beastly with delirium. Men and women reduced to monstrous vegetables, calcareous secretions, a horrendous stench. Tobino [Mario Tobino, a well known Italian writer and psychiatrist] tries to establish order in the absolute chaos of craziness. It is as if he's trying to hold back the disasters of insanity by creating a defense, a protection from insanity itself, trying to give an artistic order to the darkness, the void, the stench of the delirious. (Fellini, 2008, p. 506)

But in contrast to illness, creative work succeeds in coordinating the results of unconscious non-differentiation and conscious differentiation and so reveals the hidden order of the unconscious.

This point is well described by Anton Ehrenzweig when he stresses that the artist (unlike the insane) learns to face chaos in his work by dealing with unconscious material, and integrating it in his work as well as in his own personality. He has to elaborate primary processes of thinking that simply produce chaotic fantasy material, similar to the child's undifferentiated way of thinking. This material has to be ordered and shaped by the ego's secondary processes, a characteristic of adult life. In this way, the artist acts as a translator and interpreter for his audience (Ehrenzweig, 1967, p. 21).

Fellini and the Midlife Crisis

Jungian scholars point out that as the midlife transition begins, whether gradually or abruptly, people generally feel gripped by a sense of loss and all its emotional attendants. They are moody and experience nostalgic periods of grieving for some vaguely felt absence, a keen and growing sense of life's limits. They may undergo depression, insomnia, panic attacks, obsessions about their own death, and attempt rationalization and denial (Stein, 1983, p. 24).

At a certain psychological level, in particular in midlife, we are always in liminality, floating and unattached to identifications, betwixt and between. Liminal figures become more present somewhere in the psyche. These figures appear in dreams as the vagabond, the fool, the outcast, the prophet, the mysterious stranger, the journeyer (Stein, 1983, p. 48). These are the figures that become so vivid in Fellini dream-works. Midlife is a state of psychological liminality, when a person's sense of identity is in suspension, "feeling suspended in mid-air" to use Jung's words. One is no longer fixed to particular mental images and contents of oneself and others (Stein, 1983, pp. 8-9). In this stage the "I" is not anchored to any particular inner images, ideas, or feelings. Thus the unattached "I" floats and drifts and wanders across many former boundaries and forbidden frontiers (p.9). Liminality is created whenever the ego is unable any longer to identify fully with a former self-image, which it formed by selective attachments to specific internal patterns and basic assumptions and embodied in certain accepted and performed roles. In a series of dreams Fellini portrays himself as being stuck in a tunnel (February 1978) or in the middle of the ocean in a boat without paddles (March 1978).

Jung felt that the journey through the midlife crisis could be the foundation for a new experience of identity and integrity, based on an internal center, the Self, rather than being rooted in externals, the cues or the reinforcements derived from parental figures and other models, cultural influences, and expectations or collective pressure (Stein, 1983, p. 27). This state of mind and these figures in liminal states were persistent in Fellini's work, probably before his midlife crisis and his significant encounter with Jungian psychology and the creative work with Ernst Bernhard. It comes as no surprise that at a crucial time in the 1960s when Fellini was exactly 40 years old, he felt depressed, and turned to therapy. Bernhard encouraged Fellini to delve more deeply into the irrational and the unconscious, to remain in a state of alchemical darkness, the *nigredo*. At the same time Fellini, as Jung did before, further cultivated his interest in Eastern philosophies, parapsychology, magicians, palm readers, astrologists and mediums, structuring his intuitions and insights in this period of depression, and organizing his studies through Jungian psychology (Van Watson, 2002, p. 71). This process can be defined in Jungian terminology as a personal process of inner "dismembering" which is characterized by depression, introversion, and an emphasis on intra-psychic material, when the psychic world and the individuation of the Self take precedence over external reality, and over main everyday worries of "wife, women, money, and taxes" (Fellini, cited in Alpert, 1988, p. 156; on the Jungian meaning of the second half of life, see also Storr, 1982, ch.5).

Fellini felt he needed to distance himself from popular trends and mainstream cinematic currents. He needed to "dismember" himself in a period of chaos, and later, gradually be reborn by recreating a new identity. In one significant dream Fellini deals with his wife's death from a tumor, and a champagne toast (*brindisi*): "Tumor and champagne! A toast to death and good wishes … as though we are celebrating a rebirth!" (February 26, 1965).

In his filmography, the director looked for inner relief, which can also explain why, starting in the 1960s, Fellini moved away from the neo-realistic approach to the spoken word as a social descriptor (neo-realism) toward a more elaborate use of colors and language as symbols to give an artistic order to the darkness, the void, the stench. He fused the realistic, the symbolic and the fantastic in his later films and employed language as both a tool and an object of representation (Gaudenzi, 2002, p. 155). From the early 1960s, the universe of Fellini's movie work became less realistic, and more similar to an interplay of symbols, images and archetypes (see for example: *Otto e mezzo* (*8½*), 1963, *Giulietta degli spiriti* (*Juliet of Spirits*), 1965). Fellini's 'grotesque-ification' and symbolic metamorphosis of reality reached a climax in *La dolce vita*, whereas *8 ½* and *Giulietta degli spiriti* simply confirm this movement. The movie "*8 ½* is almost entirely composed of flashbacks in which every image is an evocative bid of baroque filigree, an inner chaotic experience" (Rossi and Lawton, 1978, p. 258).

According to Geduld, *Otto e mezzo* (*8½*) may be the last Fellini film to contain remnants of the neo-realistic tradition (1978, p.138). This movie also hints broadly at the director's personal crisis, for instance the fact that the protagonist Guido, the director's alter-ego, exhibits inner malaise, depression, disorientation, confusion and indecisiveness. For many reason he remains in a liminal state (for example staying for a long period in a spa, feeling an inner malaise, ambivalent and uncommitted in his romantic relations, blocked in his creativity as a director etc.). Like his creator, he is incapable of untangling himself from his personal social mask and inner confusion.

As stressed by Affron (1993, p. 119), the explicit subject of *8½* is the unsuccessful effort of its protagonist, Guido, to begin shooting a movie. Guido is a director in crisis, unable to make the choices necessary for the definition of his project. Scenario, casting, and décor are in a state of flux; they refuse to submit to placement or order. Guido is powerless to fix them in space, the spectacular space of the film director, a field – however shifting – of comprehensible coordinates in which a film's narrative is meant to unfold. "I am Guido" Fellini once said, when he was asked by a critic if his own problems corresponded to those of the hero of the film (Alpert, 1988, p. 167).

In his *Book of Dreams*, Fellini reports different periods of personal confusion, inertia, stagnation, and various attempts to find answers by being attuned and describing dreams, painting, using hypnagogics, active imagination (a typical Jungian technique) or consulting the Chinese *I Ching*. The Book contains reflections about *81/2* . For example a medium in a séance informs Fellini that this movie has to be made: "Open your heart…because it is like a psychoanalytical session. You will find more than you think" (Dream January 24, 1962).

A number of dreams, personal meditations, reflections and hypnagogic experiences present this leitmotiv of doubt, chaos and inner confusion, like his protagonist Guido. In chronological order, they suggest that these periods can spiral often. They represent Fellini's fear of death, and the presence of negative or repressed aspects, the *shadow* in his psyche (Ravasi Bellocchio, 2009). As he reports on January 10, 1966 and ten years later (11th May, 1976):

:

"Total inertia on all fronts. I'm not doing anything. … I am opaque, empty, deaf, unfeeling, heavy, stupid, useless…"

"In the dark dirty air, I can't fly away and reach the starry sky, because I'm tied to a big black sea serpent that is tenaciously, indissolubly bound to me and the dark scary sea".

And five years later:

one year has gone by and I haven't done a thing. Less than nothing. I've grown older, weaker, indifferent… I let myself get dragged into situations of immobility, stagnation, emptiness, recognizing them for what they were and desiring in my heart that they stayed that way. The usual psychics tell me that I'm shedding my skin and that this inertia, this lethargy I have is necessary that I HAVE TO KILL MYSELF, DISAPPEAR, BE REBORN. Whatever… (Fellini, 2008, p. 548)

Part of Jungian theory is to some extent existentialist when it stresses that in the first half of human life, better adjustment to the external world often means the healing of a neurosis (Storr, 1982, ch 5). However in almost all people over forty, there is more searching for integration and inner personal growth. Nevertheless, at this stage there can be no progress if, as the Jungian scholar von Franz points out (1999, p.22):

The persons in question do not find something within themselves that they can call the meaning of their life, a solution, or rather, *their* solution to the general problems of the times. For many, a return to their spiritual roots and a renewed understanding and better grasp of the old truth is enough. With others, however, the unconscious seems to be seeking the realization of something that has never been there before, something creatively new.

Sometimes at this stage of life a person has to come to terms with his/her "shadow" (the archetypal denied dark side of the personality), and create a new form of integration in a quest for personal meaning and wholeness. This is why Jung stressed that therapy can be beneficial for adult patients, and significant progress can be made in the second half of life. Jung, in contrast to Freud, was less deterministic and concerned about the influence of childhood on the individual, and more existentialist in his teleological emphasis on adults' quest for meaning and self-realization.

According to Jung, the shadow is simply what a person does not want to be (Samuels et al., 2003, p. 138). It includes the negative aspects of the personality, an assortment of everything unpleasant that one would like to conceal, the part that is inferior and unworthy, sometimes the projected "evil other", as well as unconscious instinctual drives or forms of aggression and sexuality (Bly, 1988). A child learns to repress or bury in the unconscious those portions of his personality that he feels are unacceptable. These parts exist, but the child prefers to keep them hidden, because the world does not accept them (Harding, 1997).

Jung repeatedly acknowledged Freud's ground-breaking work in recognizing the importance of the human shadow-side (namely the *id*) and its influence on consciousness (see discussion in Shalit, 2008, p. 81). He stressed that the shadow is part of unconscious, those unpleasant qualities we like to hide, together with the insufficiently developed functions and the contents that are not yet ripe for consciousness. With insight and good will, the shadow can, to some extent, be assimilated into the conscious personality, but resistance is often strong. However, the human being, or in Jungian terms the "hero", is alive only as long as he is tainted by the shadow. An overly-angelic perfectionist has no dangers to overcome, no struggles to endure, no weakness to suffer that makes him/her human. If there is too little vitality or too little consciousness in the hero, says Jung, the shadow becomes fatal and can later take possession of him (discussed in Shalit, 2008, p. 89). Recognition of the shadow leads to the modesty we need to acknowledge imperfection. A human relationship is not based on differentiation and perfection, but on imperfection, on what is weak, helpless and in need of support. In other words, genuinely experiencing the fulfillment of life depends on the capacity to relate to one's wounds rather than living the life of the Happy Prince in the Palace of Sans-Souci (Shalit, 2008, p. 189).

Sometimes as an adult, social morality, the facade of roles and rules of correctness, politeness and decency (the Greek mask or the *persona* in Jungian terms) elicit and preserve the repression or negation of this human aspect. The path to integration with the self must ignore the mask and come to terms with the shadow (Bly, 1988).

It is fairly predictable that the repressed shadow will return at midlife, perhaps because the structures of defense against the unconscious are less able to repel the repressed contents or because the unconscious is more strongly charged with energy than usual and is able to break through them, or a combination of these. The impulses, drives, fantasies, longings and wishes that were previously repressed make a powerful reappearance during midlife (Stein, 1983, p. 74). People may float in more than usual immediate contact with impulses and emergent unconscious contents, sometimes running amuck with impulsivity, indulging in deeply regressive urges, or succumbing to gross pleasure-seeking and to the "id" with its proclivity to perversion and its destructive potential (ibid, p. 84).

In the second half of life an adult with a stronger ego becomes like the mythical hero who approaches the encounter with what is 'bad' within him although at time as in the fifth labor of Hercules, the work seems impossible (von Franz, 1983, p. 168). The filthy task imposed on this Greek mythological hero was to clean the Augean stables of centuries of dung, "a task so enormous that the ordinary mortal would be overcome by discouragement at the mere thought of it" (ibid., p. 169). This myth suggests that man, after he has accomplished ego tasks to find a position in life (education, profession, marriage etc.) has to come to terms with dirty parts of himself, with his inner dung, his shadow, in order to achieve better integration in his psyche.

Fellini reports a dream of this nature: "I dream a lot of shit…lot of stench. Even my tie is soiled by shit" (February 15, 1975). One year later, to escape from prison Fellini dreams he has to swim under the water in horrid slime (January 6, 1976). In a another dream (March 24, 1961), Fellini has to cope with a clogged toilet full of feces and paper "I call somebody for help and with sticks… we try to open and push down all that filth, with a 600 model car, but when we try to flush it down a shitty cataclysm occurs, everything gets spewed outside…".

If the shadow is too strong, or was too strongly repressed or massively denied, and not flushed away into the sewer, the hero can be defeated and undesirable traits can take possession of the personality, soiling the decorum of a middle class director in his suit and tie, in his 600 Fiat new car (one of the symbols of Italian wealth during the sixties). As von Franz also pointed out, it would be relatively simple if the shadow could be made conscious by sincere efforts to gain insights into it and this knowledge then incorporated into our lives. Often, however, attempts at insight are useless; that is, there is such a strong drive and such an intense sense of compulsion that rational efforts are powerless: "a brick has to fall on our heads before we are able to 'turn off' the shadow's constant pushing" (1999, p. 306). To take these steps, to confront the depth of the unconscious and the negative sides of his shadow, Fellini needed courage. He had to drop his beliefs and recreate himself. One of these insights came from a dream

> Abandon the airplane,
> The preconceived ideas of intellectualness
> Get out
> Don't be afraid, the parachute will save you
> And then?
> Sinking into the water abyss,
> Down into the unconscious,
> Fish about in the unknown abyss of the sea
> And come back up.
> Descend into the unconscious. (dated February 29, 1968)

Fellini had to move into the deepest ocean, and when there, he sometimes disappeared, sometimes felt defeated, decaying, poisoned and symbolically dying. Sometimes in his dreams he reports a feeling of falling, and is terrorized into hurtling himself over a precipice (June 23, 1974). These alchemical themes appear in various periods in his dreams (Gaillard, 2009, p. 48).

Having to return from the abyss of the unconscious also means having to come to terms with monsters, with the dirt and dark sides of the psyche, the shadow. For example he has to feed monstrous animals ("half dog and half crocodile, living for a while in our kitchen") to keep them calm (December 20, 1966).

The following part of a dream, at the beginning of his therapy (December 27, 1960), is indicative of the process he was going to undertake; namely giving up his mask, and his persona as a senior manager (a director, probably with his tie) in charge of an airport sitting behind his desk and having to come to terms with a traveler with a mysterious face, from an unknown race, who elicits fear and disgust. Who is he? Where does he come from? What does he want? "This guy with Mongolian features is probably an immigrant, and clearly expects me to give him an entry permit, a visa" (my translation).

This part of the dream suggests that Fellini has to issue a visa (from the Latin root of view or seeing), an entry permit to the stranger within himself, and hence meet face to face vis-à-vis (vis, viso in Italian, visage, in French, is face in English, deriving from the same Latin root of seeing). Looking face to face is meeting with inner parts that are unknown, fearful or disgusting to the "others" in our psyche.

In another dream a young, heavy, squat and disagreeable strange boy settles down in his house without his permission, eating everything (April 20, 1967). In other dreams his house is invaded by strangers, he meets an assassin (October 8, 1961), Hitler (October, 15, 1961), ferocious tribes from the Congo (December 25, 1961), human excrement (February 16, 1962), airborne attacks of pigeon pellets (January 10, 1966), cannibals and exhumed dead from a cemetery (June 17, 1963). In many dreams he or his wife is sick or dying (for example February 26, 1965). Fellini reports his own execution, and in several dreams he is hanged (April 19, 1965), sentenced to be shot (December 10, 1976), buried alive (August 23, 1974), locked up in asylums and penitentiaries (December, 10, 1966), commits suicide (May 29, 1967), and is part of a mass suicide (August 20, 1974), experiences pus pimples ready to explode in his face (June 20, 1967), sees people beheaded (July, 19, 1967) and many instances falls or is pushed, is a victim of arson or explosions (all appear in a dream in February 1, 1968). He reports images of overcrowded elevators getting stuck (May 9, 1968), dangerous swinging (March 16, 1977) and many stories of battles, wars and revolutions (August 29, 1975), when he becomes a member of the Italian Red Brigades, the terrorist militants (May 20, 1975).

In part of a dream on April 2, 1961, Fellini feels that there is no way out of "my situation [arrested and in jail] , there is only one way to solve it, killing myself or faking a suicide… with my knife I stab myself in my stomach and .. I lose lot of blood… 'In this car there is a man who is dying', somebody exclaims" (my translation).

Fellini, (as his predecessor Jung) by expressing parts of his shadow, thus dismembers himself, the man who is dying, to be reborn in a new form, and is transformed into a spiritual guide who safely escorts us, his audience, into the unknown and takes us safely back at the end of his journey.

In the chapter on the Great Mother, the theme of being devoured by the black serpent of the unconscious (related to mother earth and the need to being reborn or refreshed by her body), is shown to be recurrent in Fellini's work, not only as part of his mid-life crisis.

Fellini as a person was a positive Hero, who was non-conformist, and was attracted by the unconscious and supernatural wild world of the shadow. He was able to cross the magical threshold of the unconscious and transit into a sphere of rebirth. He was able to kill the sea serpent again and again. As an adult he came to terms and better integrated his inner shadow. He undertakes the perilous journey into the darkness by descending, either intentionally or unintentionally, "into the crooked lanes of his own spiritual labyrinth, he soon finds himself in a landscape of symbolical figures… this is the process of dissolving, transcending, or transmuting the infantile images of our personal past" (Campbell, 1968, p. 101).

In many myths, the idea that crossing the magical threshold is a point of transit into a sphere of pain, loss, dismemberment, cleansing of decaying filth, dying, and rebirth is symbolized by the universal maternal womb or the image of the stench of the belly of a fish (in one of Fellini's dreams, dated October 31, 1961, its belly is full of trinitrotoluene, an explosive mixture). The hero, instead of conquering or conciliating the power of the threshold, is swallowed into the unknown, and seems to have died. This popular motif emphasizes that crossing the threshold is a form of self annihilation. Instead of passing outward, beyond the confines of the visible world, the hero goes inward, to be born again (Campbell, 1968, p. 90-1). Allegorically entering a temple and the hero diving into the jaws of the whale are identical adventures, both denoting, pictorially, the life-centering, life-renewing act after dangerous ordeals (Campbell, 1968, p. 92).

Thus if anyone – in whatever society – undertakes for himself the perilous journey into the darkness by descending, either intentionally or unintentionally, into the crooked lanes of his own spiritual labyrinth, he soon finds himself in a landscape of symbolic figures: "this is the process of dissolving, transcending, or transmuting the infantile images of our personal past" (Campbell, 1968, p. 101).

Chapter 2

HERMES IN FELLINI'S LIFE

THE GOD OF MOVEMENT

Rabbinical Jewish tradition tells a story about four Sages, Ben Azzai, Ben Zoma, Acher and Rabbi Akiva, who entered the Secret Garden (in Hebrew the *Pardes*, literally the orchard) and ascended to the secret knowledge of heaven by utilizing the Divine Name in order to achieve spiritual elevation (Talmud, Hagiga14b). Ben Azzai gazed into the heavens and died. Ben Zoma gazed and went mad. Acher became a heretic. Only Rabbi Akiva entered in peace and left in peace.

This story is warning to those who, even properly prepared, wish to learn the absolute truth and explore into the secret knowledge of the Holy Scriptures, gaze into the Heavens or approach the depths of the unknown, the uncanny and the secret of unconscious (in Hebrew the *sod*, which includes the Jewish Kabbalah). Fellini believed that the ascent into the world of the absolute is best elicited by artists and psychologists. Today's rational and alienating life styles force many people to seek the unexplainable, the sacred or the unconscious. Many consider it a step in a process of personal growth and development, and a way to achieve new insights about the world and themselves. But it is also dangerous ordeal when the person is not ready:

> for the artist it is an entry full of treasures where you can grab all the stories, like a treasure in the depth of the sea or in a tunnel in which you have to overcome monsters, gatekeepers, or dragons (Fellini quoted in Pettigrew, 1994, p. 57, my translation).

In his symbolic style Fellini warns us that the creative path of the artist has many pitfalls where he is exposed to dangers in the form of "satanic hell keepers". The abyss is not always demiurgic, it can dismember and kill. However, Fellini differed from creative but troubled artists like Van Gogh, Baudelaire, Poe, and Rimbaud, who in their personal crises paid a very high price for having approached certain truths too early and without sufficient inner strength or maturity, or without the aid of a spiritual guide or knowledge of psychoanalysis (ibid, p. 57-58). Fellini, like Rabbi Akiva, entered into this secret world in peace (despite difficult ordeals) and left in peace, and was able to bring vital archetypical images and emotions from there to humankind. This part of Fellini is present in all his films: "he is ever present when he tells us that film (ambiguously anchored to external reality) is an art of memory, through which one can narrate only one's own memories, fantasies, and obsessions" (Eco, 1993, p. 294).

Jungian scholars typically begin any exegesis with mythology, to analyze the archetypal god who may be considered the ancestor and protector of a person, such as Fellini, the mythical and benevolent Guide who can move from dizzying heights to the watery abyss of the unconscious and be reborn again. The Greek god Hermes (the Roman Mercurius/Mercury) appears to apply best to Fellini not only because his attributes shed light on many characteristics of Fellini's personality, but also because of the director's style of work, his screenplays and his protagonists, as well as the way he safely escorts his audience and shares his "big dreams". Fellini is like a herald, a messenger, a translator, an interpreter of different layers of reality (typical qualities of Hermes) whose works attempt to cause an inner change in our personal lives, sometimes in a mocking, cunning and subversive way.

Linking Hermes with Fellini is suggestive of the nature of his impact. The god Hermes, as stressed by Kerenyi, corresponds to a reality or at least to the reality of the soul, a way of being, an *idea*, something beyond our historical vision (1990, p. 5): "for if we are to have success in reviving the god's image in its fullness, we must be prepared not only for what is immediately intelligible, but also for what is strangely uncanny".

Hermes/Mercurius was quicksilver. He was the essence, fluid or principle behind or within quicksilver -- that indefinable, fascinating, irritating, and elusive thing which attracts an unconscious projection (Jung, 1970, p. 211). The metal associated with Hermes is mercury. The alchemists called it quicksilver or liquid silver because of its liveliness, its malleability and its capacity to transform itself (Paris, 1990, p.109). Hermes is dual, and his main characteristic is duplicity. It is said that he runs round the earth and enjoys equally the company of the good and the wicked (Jung, 1970, p. 217), masculine and feminine, young and old. Hermes was the god of curiosity and movement, roads and entries, a wayfarer and a safe guide. Hermes was audacious, innocent, cunning, wise, phallic, magical, shameless, delightful, provocative, equivocal, slippery, elusive, dual, playful, surprising and protecting (Yeoman, 1998, p. 36-38). Many of these attributes characterized Fellini's personality and many of his male protagonists as well.

Hermes is evasive and ambiguous, as quicksilver cannot be confined to notions that are alien to its own mercurial ways. It is the unconscious itself, which in part resists being boxed into fixed temporal contexts and causal sequences but always keeps a measure of freedom to float and to drift, to pass through the keyholes of our psychological shelters.

Hermes does not possess a distinct personality. He is unknown, a wild thing in the world, without a rank in the social structure and hierarchy, outside standard ways of thinking, feeling and behaving. He is never influenced by group pressure, conformism, ideologies, conditioning or uncritical learning. Probably Umberto Eco was the first to note Fellini's similarity to Hermes: "three times as great as Hermes-Thoth always transcends, with his ship, what the external world would like to impose upon his internal world, and upon the voracity of his nostalgia" (Eco, 1993, p. 294).

Fellini's character and creations, like Hermes, mark him as strikingly different from all the (Olympian) directors of his epoch. Fellini the anti-conformist is a quicksilver who cannot be assigned o political or social frameworks or any artistic genre or esthetic pigeon-hole. He was neither realist nor neo-realist, neither Fascist nor Catholic, neither Marxist nor post-modernist. He was neither an intellectual nor an anarchist, neither chauvinist nor feminist. He quickly moved through many layers of reality. In his work he opposed "a spiritual, magical, and religious conscience that participates in the mystery of the universe" (Calvino, 1993, p. 27). Fellini was a brave journeyer, like Hermes, and a guide of wayfarers among his public.

In older works of art, Hermes often appears wearing a traveler's hat. His pace is always swift. The speed which distinguishes him is symbolized by the wings of his hat. He possesses golden sandals with which he can fly like the wind over land and sea. This is an apt description of his nature (Otto, 1955, p. 114). Jung identifies the spiritual Hermes with the winged youth who stands for everything that is winged in the psyche or that would like to sprout wings, and is simultaneously a representation of autonomous creativity and the impulse to evade the restrictions and confinement of laws, circumstances, responsibility and destiny (Yeoman, 1998, p. 39).

These traits are very characteristic of Fellini. Two extras who watched Fellini on the stage, when directing *Satyricon* (in Bachman's *Ciao Federico!* 1969) noted:

> "It is all an illusion… He (Fellini) suddenly looks up, you see his brain just flying over hills, reefs… over the sea, and comes back and goes on."
>
> "I think he is going into a different world of fantasy, it is not the world we live in. He doesn't need it".

Fellini was never static (even under the influence of LSD), but like Hermes, the god of the roads, he never kowtowed to any fashion, political party, artistic school or ideology. He was the man of his movies, and followed his own truth, and knew what he wanted to accomplish very early on in life. He moved to Rome to enroll in law school, which is what his parents wanted him to do. This was his first and last day he ever set foot in the Rome School of Law. He rapidly failed to live up to *medio borghese* expectations, at a time when such a step took strength and courage. He, like Hermes, did not work for grades or awards or others' expectations. He, as those influenced by Hermes, was successful when the work itself attracted him, elicited his creativity (Shinoda Bolen, 1989), and satisfied his need to fly over hills and reefs. As Hermes he was the nimble and agile god who "always evaded lumbering attempts to grasp him" (Otto, 1955, p. 107). Fellini stated on different occasions that he was not a man who approved of definitions, because "labels belong on luggage as far as I'm concerned, they don't mean anything in art" (cited in Bondanella, 1992, p. xix).

In many dreams and hypnagogic experiences he flies or vibrates, like Hermes, moving through different layers of life and reality. Missiles, airplanes, rockets and jets frequently appear in his dreams:

In a dream dated March, 20, 1975 he writes:

> I'm on a big airliner that is landing right smack in the middle of a city at extremely high speed. I see the facades of buildings along the large tree-lined street where the airplane's wheels are about to touch down flash by outside the little window of the jet. At high speed, its wings brush the windows, building doors, trees. The experience is at once terrifying and exhilarating. I want to meet, compliment, applaud the extraordinary pilot capable of such an achievement. And suddenly I find myself along with all the passengers suspended in a little metal chair shaped like a basket, outside the plane on the wings, where I have a better view of the prodigious landing. The airplane has touched down, its speed has

> diminished, may be the airport is down there at the end of the street. One wing clips the façade of a building, but nothing dangerous happens because the wing folds gently back like an elbow. I wasn't afraid, but I hear laughter around me as though it was all a big joke on me. Now the captain comes out of the body of the plane. He's a handsome man, strong, tanned, and looks at me, smiling and entertained. (Fellini,2008, p. 526).

Is the captain Hermes, his personal guide, or an inner part of him-Self? Fellini talks about a feeling of vibrating, taking off, or the ground moving up and down, as a memory of his hypnagogic experiences in childhood, and also in dreams. This occurs in a dream dated September 9, 1978.

The same old vibrations and the vertical ascent of my body toward a night sky. I fly and know that I am once again living through this mysterious experience. (Fellini, 2008, p. 540):

> Sometimes there is a sequel with a different form of vertical and horizontal movement (p. 512):

> Big airplanes taking off; I can see a highway. I realize that alongside the highway in question there's another highway. I need to get onto that one and then everything will be all right.

There is a great deal of verticality in his movement and images, where airplanes (and airports), space ships and incredibly beautiful and fantastic missiles appear (for example in a dream dated March 1, 1980).Sometimes, like Hermes, during these vibrations ("what bliss") he is also invisible (February 22, 1962).

Hermes has winged shoes and an invisibility cap which certainly involves magic (Otto, 1955, p. 106). Hermes is not only the master of magic words; he also has a magic wand. His most ancient and most typical attribute was a rod, about the length of a man's arm, surmounted by a convolution best described as a figure eight. Hermes with his magical staff induces drowsiness and awakens sleepers – he is a dream-maker and ruler of dreams (Yeoman, 1998, p. 38). Fellini mostly appears in a variety of caps and with his inseparable megaphone, his modern magic rod which gives him authority, as the *director*, to conduct his scenes and later to lead his audience on journeys into the magic of his own *terra incognita,* his own dreamlike works.

HERMES, AND FELLINI: GUIDE OF THE SOULS ON A DIFFERENT LEVEL OF REALITY

Hermes is the Roman Mercury, the nimble messenger of the Olympic gods, who was able to move between different layers of reality, from Olympus to Hades, the realm of Death and back again: "in this gloomy sphere also Hermes' activity has two directions: he not only leads downward but also upward. So in the Homeric Hymn to Demeter, he brings Persephone back from the realm of the dead" (Otto, 1955, p. 113).

Hermes was the god who accompanied the souls of the dead and was able to move between polarities, not only heaven and earth, the divine and human realm, but also between death and life, night and day, the feminine and the masculine, the depths of sleep and psychic movement and the reality of the ego. He was “the one who leads souls away and leads them back” (Kerenyi, 1990, p. 69). In Greek mythology this figure which guides the soul at times of initiation or transition (in dying), and endows a sense of ultimate purpose, calling or destiny. The one that connects the ego and the unconscious is also known as the psychopomp (Samuels and oth. 2003, pp. 122-123). As a good guide, Hermes was a friendly god to humankind (Shinoda Bolen, 1989).

The theme of death and rebirth, so specific to Hermes in his role as escort of the souls appears in many Fellini movies and dreams. For example (dream dated April 19, 1982, Fellini, 2008, p. 550): “Between two corpses, I know I have to plant basil between their fingers, to attempt resurrection”.

And April 26, 1977:

> At the cemetery several workers unearth a coffin and use ropes to raise it up out of its tomb. Through a pane of glass, like a little window, on the side I glimpse a female figure who turns her perfectly conserved head. She's alive! It's Adriana from film editing, who smiles, entertained, as if she was expecting this liberation.

In another dream Fellini connects these worlds, to communicate with dead people, the way Guido in *8½* communicated with his dead parents (dream dated February 24, 1961):

> A big girl who might be a maid and even a part-time prostitute asks me for a letter of recommendation so that she can find a job...She tells me she is in continuous communication with her dead father, she can call him up and talk to him at any time, and asks him for advice on even the smallest things. I feel a deep sympathy for this big girl, I believe what she

is telling me. I know it's true... a girl like you doesn't need any letter of recommendation! I smile at her moved.

Fellini was a *psychopomp* in his own way. With his geniality, creativity and simplicity he could report what he had encountered during his journey and share his reflections on death (Ravasi Bellocchio, 2009). He did so in "a retrograde stylistic fashion that corresponds to a childish, disembodied, and pre-cinematographic visualization of 'another' world" (Calvino, 1993, p. 27). He had a friendly, spontaneous and easy manner, stating that in fact "spontaneity is the secret of life" (Fellini in Pettigrew, 1994, p. 75), when he was able to trust his instinct and native talent, with lyrical and irrational infantilism (Pasolini, 1993, p. 106-107). But like an innocent child he was also a sage or a wise shaman. Fellini used his personal trajectory to instruct us and to provide reassurance, speaking about life (and its secrets) and death in extremely simple and protective terms (Pettigrew, 1994, pp. 80-81).

God of the Road and Border Crosser

Hermes is the God of the road; his pillar was a heap of stones by the wayside, to which every passer-by piously contributed. This gave him his name, for there can be no doubt the Hermes means "he of the stone heap" (in Greek *herma*). As a newborn he escaped from his cradle, and went to steal his brother (Apollo's) cattle. Hermes earned what he deserved using his creativity and imagination from the very first day of his birth. As Rafael Lopez-Pedraza notes, on the day Hermes was born, a very cunning thief also emerged, perhaps one of the earliest kinds of cattle robbers (2003, p. 58). During his early career, a number of interesting stories circulated about Fellini that were either confirmed during interviews with him or at least not denied including the idea that he was born on a train; that he ran away to join the circus in 1927 which supposedly explains his later interest in clowns (Bondanella, 1992, p. 282). Fellini's biographer Tullio Kezich denies all these rumors, but they add something of Hermes's nature to the director: being born *on* the road, escaping from home (like the newborn Hermes escaping from his cradle) at an early age, attracted by a world of jesters and tricksters who are constantly on the move. Probably Fellini as a child ran away from home. The first time, at the age of seven he tried to join the circus, motivated by the simple desire to belong to the circus, and travel from place to place after having been to a performance. As Kezich stressed "for that reason, one might almost be justified in saying that in one form or another, the first escape really did occur… although it didn't last a couple of days; it lasted a lifetime" (2006, p. 9).

In his movie *Clowns,* Fellini's reenacts his childhood fascination with the circus, where the big top is quickly erected outside his bedroom windows. In this way Fellini made his biography come true. Clowns come and go out of the blue. His mother's warning that he might be kidnapped by gypsies who are constantly on the road (like his Zampanò and Gelsomina in *La strada*), can be seen as a prophecy. His mother was right in her warning because Federico remained captivated by this world of vagrants throughout his life. In an interview, Fellini recalled that

> as a child I was attracted by artists, those with long hair, who didn't wash, with colorful dresses, with beautiful girls, who eat when they want…like vagrants… it was a kind of childish rebellion against laws, taboos, the roles imposed by the house or the school, the Catholic church and fascism. (Pettigrew, 1994, p. 25-26, my translation)

Vagrants, under the protection of Hermes, are the kings of the road. Mercury, in alchemy, is the symbol of the conjunction of opposites, heaven and earth, as well the feminine and the masculine, achieved by crossing borders or thresholds. Fellini, like Hermes, was involved in a repetitive attempt to search for the union of opposites (for example androgyny), in a quest for the Center, a place where heaven, earth and hell meet. The Center is the place where creation originates, not only the creation of the world, but also the creation of man. As in the Tibetan mandala, alchemy and Jungian archetypical psychology, the Center also means the original wholeness of the self, the conjunction of opposites. As Mircea Eliade noted

> The road leading to the center is a difficult road… [for] the seeker for the road to the self, to the center of his being, and so on. The road is arduous, fraught with perils, because it is in fact, a rite of the passage from the profane to the sacred, from the ephemeral and illusory to reality and eternity, from death to life, from man to divinity. Attaining the center is equivalent to a consecration, an initiation; yesterday's profane and illusory existence gives way to a new, to a life that is real, enduring, and effective. (1959, p. 18):

The road leading to the center is a difficult road, and in many of Fellini's movies the protagonists move without any clear goal or purpose, without a beginning or an end. Chaos and circularity are found instead of clarity and linearity (for instance, *La strada*, the Road). In other movies his protagonists are stuck in their inner infernal traffic jam, and sometimes, in the depictions of Rome, the Eternal City, they are slowly moving along its external highways (*Roma, Toby Dammit*). Other heroes cannot create any direction out of chaos, or give birth (in Italian "dare alla luce" means also giving life, giving light out of chaos). This theme is central to *8½*, and to Guido's creative stagnation. The hero in this film cannot find his inner central balance.

God of Crafts, Art, Communication, Language and Interpretation

The relationship between primitive craftsmanship and magic, although difficult to define, is admittedly a close one. Primitive magic is a technology of sorts. Its aim is the manipulation of the external world. The primitive craftsman supplements his technique with magical practices, and success at his craft is taken to indicate possession of magical powers. Hermes the craftsman is celebrated in myths of various types. In some he is described as an inventor; in the Homeric hymn the lyre, the rustic pipe, and the art of making fire are all said to be his discoveries (Brown, 1990, p. 21). Hermes was familiar with the art of divination, the will of God, was an expert in "sound making", and was a singer, a bard, the source of song and poetry in the intoned formulae of magical incantation (Brown, 1990, p. 25-29). Typical epithets for Hermes are "crafty" and "ingenious" (Otto, 1955, p. 104).

Fellini is *the man* of the art of movies (Eco, 1993, p. 293), for whom creation was always a natural part of his personal life. Like Hermes he did not like to work according to an instruction manual but rather invented technical solutions or creative short-cuts to his work (Shinoda Bolen, 1989). Fellini also invented new linguistic terms. For example words like *vitelloni* (today a synonym for a Mama's boy), *dolce vita* and *paparazzo* were coined by Fellini. Other cryptic words were later understood by the public, like Asa-NIsi-MAsa= ANIMA, an acrostic reminiscent of his childhood (in *Otto e mezzo*).

There is something magical in Hermes as well in Fellini. Their craft is never represented as a rational device, but as a manifestation of magic power with a magic wand. Even in the myth of the cattle theft, in which Hermes is a thief rather than trickster, his success at stealing is attributed to magic. In the 20th century as well, thieves have been known to try to supplement their technique with magic (Brown, 1990, p. 11).

It makes sense that Hermes was considered the inventor of language. Hermes is also the language *interpreter*, a linguistic mediator (in the field of *herme*neutics for example), and not only verbally. By nature he is the begetter and conveyor of clarity, a god of exposition and interpretation which seeks and in his spirit is led to the deepest mysteries (Kerenyi, 1990, p. 88). Fellini, as a person with obvious talents in the field of mass communication, could feel at one with this archetype, because a modern Hermes can fly easily over the radio, TV painting or writing (Shinoda Bolen, 1989). He can surf the media.

THE TRICKSTER

Hermes is also a trickster who impudently lies and steals. According to Greek mythology he was a child "of many a wily and cunning council, a robber, a driver of the cattle, a captain of raiders, a watcher of the night, a thief at the gates" (Kerenyi, 1990, p. 20). At the Hermes festival in ancient Crete, the lowest caste, the slaves, were momentarily elevated and served by their masters. At another festival the populace was allowed to steal and commit highway robbery. The theme of the carnival and other festivals (so frequent in Fellini movies) may also be related to the Hermes archetype. This personality trait can have also positive implications. As Brown points out

> Depending on the historical circumstances, the trickster may evolve into any one of such contrasting figures as a benevolent culture hero nearly indistinguishable from the Supreme God, a demiurge in strong opposition to the heavenly powers, a king of devils counteracting the creator in every possible way, a messenger and mediator between gods and men, or merely a Puckish figure, the hero of comical stories. (1990, p. 46)

Being a trickster also gives a person the ability to understand what happens in other people's minds. Like a detective, the trickster can anticipate other people's intentions and solve problems in a creative and unusual way. Hermes was the cunning trickster, the hero of stealthy appropriation (Brown, 1990, p. 7) "when the Greek tragedians describe Hermes as 'tricky' or as 'the trickster', they have in mind not a patron of theft or any other type of misappropriation, but a guileful patron of stealthy action in general, of deception and sexual seduction in particular".

Making movies is an art of deception par excellence. Fellini seems to have been blessed with a precocious talent for gags, sketches, comic relief and caricatures. In his creations he was capable of subverting the religious, social and political order, and as an artist, to be pardoned. The same can be said about his sexual seductive talent. In a wry comment, Fellini said about himself: "I am a liar, but an honest one. People reproach me for not always telling the same story in the same way. But this happens because I've invented the whole tale from the start and it seems boring to me and unkind to other people to repeat myself" (Fellini, 1976, p. 49). When encountering this part of himself in a dream (November 29, 1974), Fellini said he could not rely on a person like that, with his roguish smile (*sorriso da cialtrone*) and treacherous glance (*sguardo infido*).

Fellini, blessed by Hermes, who is also the god of windfalls and luck, came to Rome and started from nothing, had a great career and made a fortune. In Rimini and in Rome, after his third and definitive escape from his "maternal cradle", he started his career inventing cartoons, one-liner gags and illustrating them with clever, *tricky* sketches.

> To Hermes, Olympus is where he belongs and the theft of cattle is an act of justice! But getting the goods is only a first step. The goods must then be recognized as his; his ownership must be seen as legitimate. This way of thinking applies to many a self-made man, and to those parvenus who choose to forget their origins. Their biographies illustrate the Hermes myth: the self-made man decided in his youth that the gates of some Olympus should be open to him, that justice should be done to his genius without his worrying too much about scruples. (Paris, 1990, p. 73)

Fellini the artist is fundamentally a transgressor and as such can also be a revolutionary. He is a caricaturist by nature, attracted by the carnivalesque, the grotesque, the hybrid and whatever disrespected or subverted well ordered society, the family, the state and the church. The grotesque characterizes his personality. It is a hybrid, a mixture of different components, lacking uniformity, coherence or the absolute. It is typified by a lack of differences, a lack of a clear identity. The grotesque is lawless, unconventional and surprising, and may repulse because its elements do not jibe. For this reason the grotesque is a threat to Judeo-Christian culture which respects binary order, dual morality (holy and profane, pure and impure, good and bad, licit and illicit, subject and object, inside and outside, left and right, up and down, past, present and future, male and female, life and death etc.; see discussion in Kuryluk, 1987). The hybrid, as part of the grotesque, can also include a confusion in the borders and laws of time, gender distinctions, chronology, the natural evolution of events, the laws of linearity (Harpham, 1982). Therefore it causes confusion; it is either wonderful or monstrous, ridiculous or terrible (Bakhtin, 1965; Kayser, 1963).

In a séance session Fellini was said to be a person "having a circumfused nature" (Fellini, 2008, p. 489). *Circonfuso* is a rare word in both Italian and English which means "being pervaded by air, light and similar". Doubtless these attributes fit Fellini's character. However as a director he exemplified both the *circum*, a prefix akin to circus (the Latin root means 'ring') and the confused.

The theme of thieving and cheating (*Il bidone, I vitelloni, Le notti di Cabiria*), and marital infidelity is recurrent in Fellini's dreams and filmography (*Luci del varietà, La strada, The white sheik, Giulietta degli spiriti, 81/2, Satyricon, La dolce vita, La città delle donne*). His personal capacity to invent, distort reality, to wink, to use humor, to be amusing, were all expressed with artistic talent that enabled him, a puckish director, to be excused and pardoned. Fellini's cynicism and sarcasm were condoned by the authorities (the fascist regime despite his cynical skepticism and long hair, the church, the political establishment, the Italian moral right, and also his wife, despite his libertine romantic affairs). Like Hermes's lies, which were accompanied by his most guileless face, which enabled him to swear falsely to his brother Apollo to clear himself of the suspicion of cattle rustling, making his omniscient father Zeus smile benevolently, Fellini's most subversive and critical movie about the political establishment, *Prova d'orchestra*, was previewed, on its first release, in the *sancta sanctorum* of the political establishment, in the presence of the President of the Republic Sandro Pertini. Fellini, who waged a constant war against private channels and their lack of respect for artistic work interrupted by their vulgar advertisements (see for example *Ginger e Fred*), became involved in a few short advertisements, one with a veiled reference to oral sexuality (for Barilla food company). This act is similar to the subterfuge of the Trojan Horse, invented by Ulysses.

Even as a child, Fellini had the ability to create worlds with his imagination, and to destroy the order of rationality through ruse. As a formidable craftsman he utilized these capacities to his own advantage. His mother, as reported in Bachman's *Ciao Federico!* commented: "What can I tell you. From the age of ten he loved puppet theatre. He dressed them like a tailor… he performed for the kids, and charged a penny each".

Fellini was attracted by the subversive character of clowns: "the ambassadors of my profession. In my childhood they were the premiere image of disrespect" (cited in Free, 1973, p. 219). In the clown he found the grotesque the irrational aspect of man; he stands for the instinct, for whatever is rebellious in each one of us and whatever stands up to the established order of things. He is a caricature of man's childish and animal aspects, the mocker and the mocked. The clown is a mirror in which man sees himself in a grotesque, deformed, ridiculous image. He is man's shadow. (quoted in Bondanella, 1992, p. 186)

As stressed by Stoddart

> The circus, and especially the clowns, mirror the loss of order and limitation that defines the mental asylum's inhabitants; yet in Fellini's terms the circus has license not to have to keep inside fixed bounds and in fact to celebrate those same deficiencies for which the asylum patients have been confined. The clowns *perform* the insanity that those in the asylum *experience*. (2002, p. 55)

And finally, Free notes that the grotesque in art was originally a mode of rebellion (1973, p. 217).

Fellini drew many parallels between grotesque figures in his childhood town and actors in the circus, suggesting that the virtual reality of the circus is not distinct from aspects of the real world. Similar to the figures in his real life that made Rimini a living circus, his journey into the biography of previous actors in a French circus school and his investigation of their personal lives reveals how human and sometimes tragic these characters are ("it is difficult to get older").

Pranks, sexual allusions, and acts that challenge the patriarchal and fascist order (for example the scene of a youth blowing a raspberry at the local stationmaster in *Clowns*) introduce what would later become his monumental memories in *Amarcord*. The village idiot, the pathetic dandy, a crazy midget nun who spends half of her time in the convent (the place of order), half in the asylum (the place of chaos), a Fascist officer who absurdly and purposeless goes round and round in his motorcycle sidecar, a crowd of village loafers "all are grotesque versions of humanity; all are caricatures" (Free, 1973, p. 222). Fellini himself felt like a clown, and in so doing he mocked himself and us as well. In a dream dated February 4, 1961:

> Franco Franchi and Ciccio Ingrassia [two famous Italian comic actors], with their faces heavily made-up in a small bar on the outskirts of the city. I am made up like a clown too, and that's how I show up in Federiz's offices, which are turned upside down for renovations… I try to take off my chalky make-up in front of a mirror but the flesh flakes off

together with the greasepaint, a pulp of face paint and blood from around my eyes smears my hand...

In *Clowns* he manipulates the act in the ring and emerges as the ultimate grotesque figure in the performance, the creator who rebels against absurdity by creating the ultimately absurd performance in which he himself is the star clown (Free, 1973, p. 223). In the movie, a reporter asks Fellini, "what is the meaning of all this?" Before Fellini can answer this intellectual question, a bucket thrown from the ring falls on his head. Another falls on the reporter, silencing them both: "the author of the spectacle is thus mocked by his own creation. The intellectual idea of 'meaning' in the sense of an explication of the comic action into ideas is ridiculed" (Free, 1973, p. 225).

MERCURY AND HIS HERMETIC VESSEL

In alchemy, Mercury (the Greek Hermes) needed to intervene to unite opposites. The end product of his alchemical work was to transform the two opposing elements into one another, until they converged on a central point finally merging into a new substance. On a more profound level, the alchemist reflects both the alchemical process and the means behind the process; the alchemical process was tantamount to both self-knowledge and to the knowledge of the divine, and the goal of the alchemical process was somehow equivalent to the starting point, the *prima materia.* The hermetic vessel (in Latin the *vas hermeticum*) may be depicted as the retorts or smelting furnace in which the transformation takes place with fire and water. This vessel was seen as a symbolic Grail, signifying the womb of matter, a universal vessel of all transformations (Walker, 1983, p. 1043).

For alchemists this vessel was important because of its special connections to both the basic *prima materia* of the alchemical work (*opus*) and its outcome, the conjunction of opposites and the creation of gold or the philosophical stone. It was in the furnace, varying in size to render different degrees of heat, where the main alchemical processes occurred. The vessel was considered marvelous and had to be completely round to imitate the spiral cosmos, so that the influence of the stars might contribute to a successful outcome. This space was also depicted as the baptismal font, the vessel of nature or uterus from which the miraculous stone (*lapis*), would be created. This vessel is also a mystical concept, and for Jungians, a space for inner creativity and transformation.

There are some similarities between the alchemical vessel (Jung's Tower, located in Bollingen), and Fellini's movie studio, located in Cinecittà, in Rome. It was the workshop where Fellini created his *opus magna.* In the prologue to his movie *Intervista* (*Interview*, 1987), he escorts us down one of his paths to connect with this collective unconscious experience by sharing a personal dream (again with a theme of transportation and verticality between layers of consciousness):

> I was in a dark, disturbing, but also familiar environment. I was slowly moving in the dark and my hands were touching a never ending wall. Now being older and heavier, it was an effort for me to take off from the ground, but finally I could manage it, and I found myself hovering at very high altitude. And the landscape I was seeing between dispelled clouds, what was it? The University Campus?... It was Cinecittà!

Fellini, like Hermes, is capable of moving from earth to heaven, and Cinecittà was not only Fellini's main place of work, in a sense a little "fortress" or an "alibi", but also his alchemical workshop, his personal temple, his sanctuary, his Greek *temenos*, the "Tower" of Jung, where he could combine different and opposite alchemical materials to brew a new creation, from earth to heaven. This place elicited extraordinary encounters with the personal and collective aspects of the unconscious, the universal psyche and its central archetypes: "at times Cinecittà seems to be a hospital, a sanatorium, a convalescent home" (quoted in Angelucci, 1993, p. 181). In fact the Asclepian *temenos* is also a place of healing. In *Interview* we are told that Cinecittà's archives (*cineteca*), conserve the "memory of itself", in other words the knowledge and memory of all humankind. This area can still grow nutritious crops from its soil, even in a polluted metropolitan zone (in *Interview* it is chicory).

Cinecittà, the huge Italian workshop of film making, becomes a strong vessel for Fellini, a container and a creator of everything, like our collective unconscious.

For Fellini this place was a city that manufactures dreams and the opportunity to stage and deliver the world of the unconscious to the public. This world is a new dimension of space and time, where opposites can unite and create new material, an alchemical conjunction. On the way to this "city", we can meet elephants, American Indian tribes, alpine watcrfalls, and old-fashioned scenes with divas or Maharaja's palaces (in *Interview*). Like in dreams, everything is possible: "naturally, none of these sights could possibly be found near Rome, but in the cinema, Fellini is informing us, anything the mind can imagine is possible" (Bondanella, 1992, p. 209).

The audience, like the young hero who plays young Fellini as a journalist, can stay wonderstruck and leave this place with a newly inspired level of consciousness, in a new dream-like state. As Fellini himself said in an interview, the workshop is not just a place of work, but, as was the case for alchemists, a place of inner transformation, a psychological hearth:

> I don't stay at Cinecittà. I live there. My experience, my journeys, my friendships and my relations begin and end in the studios of Cinecittà. Everything which exists outside the gates of Cinecittà are tributaries – certainly un-substitutable, a marvelous and enormous repository to visit, to loot and to carry back to Cinecittà, greedily, tirelessly. I don't know if all this is a privilege or slavery, but it's my way of being (quoted in Angelucci, 1993, p. 180).

As the hermetic vessel inside the larger workshop devoted to alchemy, for Fellini "the ideal place… is Theater 5 in Cinecittà when it's empty. Total emotion, trembling ecstasy is what I feel there in that empty studio – a space to fill up, a world to create" (quoted in Bondanella, 1992, p. 211). This hearth becomes the symbol of his soul, and his movies become his *opus magna*. Kezich writes that for some time the director had a private apartment inside Cinecittà (2006, p. 290). There he used to live "like an athlete in training, waking at seven to exercise and getting massages… like an artisan who's discovered that the meaning of life lies in doing his job well".

Chapter 3

HERMES IN FELLINI'S WORK

CONJUNCTION OF SEXUAL OPPOSITES

It is always a challenge to depict the figure of Hermes because of his dual complexity. Hermes has a borderline nature or being. This is exemplified in his dual existence: half female and half male, half in a mental institution and half outside, half neurotic with psychotic spells, either as an expression of Hermes' pathology or as a manifestation of his true essence. This is something we have all experienced. It is the feeling of being half-sick, half-healed as though our lives were travelling down that road between sickness and healing (Lopez-Pedraza, 2003, p. 25-26).

Many attributes of Hermes are found in the figure of the hermaphrodite, which translates them into a complex language of its own, a rare, but quintessential conjunction of opposites. According to Jungian scholars, the hermaphrodite psychology in the deepest sense is the beginning of real psychology. This makes sense if we see the hermaphrodite as a specific consciousness in itself, a basic reality of life which makes the psyche possible; i.e., man and woman, male and female, animus and anima, in sum an essential integration of opposites of humankind. The hermaphrodite introduces us to the complexities of the masculine and the feminine within a unique symmetrical image (Lopez-Pedraza, 2003, p. 39-40). On the one hand s/he is bisexual, with an obscure pathology, and on the other, s/he is a psychic mover (p. 44).

In the ancient Greek tradition, the hermaphrodite within the house represents the origin or the source: s/he represents the primal condition restored in marriage that precedes even the genesis and the generation of souls. Thus widows went to pray to the hermaphrodite in a small Attic temple dedicated to him to beg for restoration of that condition which is far more than transient happiness in love or mere amorous union. It is a unique union of opposites. Even today the Greeks call a married couple *to androgyno*, "the androgene" (Kerenyi, 1990, p. 83).

Hermes shares with Aphrodite and Demeter the honor of being invoked when fertility is at stake, either with couples or with flocks and herds (Paris, 1990, p. 107).

In Fellini's works, features of hermaphrodites can be found in the Austrian Archduke in *E la nave va* (*And the ship sails on*). He/she is a very powerful personality, escorted and protected by many functionaries. When interviewed, his/her answers are short, vague, and difficult to translate and understand. He is *Hermetic*, cryptic like an ancient oracle. "We are on the edge of a crater", he says days before the beginning of First World War. But his/her powerful presence can resolve dangerous situations, for instance when the Italian ship is under attack from an Austrian battleship.

Another hermaphrodite, in Fellini's *Satyricon* is an albino, an ageless child. Again he is an oracle, a demi-god, who has the capacity to heal. But he/she has to be protected by old wise men. He/she must remain in a cave, not be exposed to the sun, in a damp place beside a pool. The hermaphrodite, portrayed as a frail child, is worshipped in a very odd way by the most freakish children of the god. The two young male anti-heroes of the movie – Encolpio and Ascilto – carry out the ultimate concretization of stealing this strange healing power as a fetish ad for picaresque profit, an act that inevitably leads to its destruction, the death of the child, and their future unlucky fortunes.

The decision to steal and possess him/her to capture the offerings given to him/her by the sick, ceases with the death of the hermaphrodite. This also means that a mere state of conjunction between Hermes and Aphrodite (Hermaphrodite) is a rarity, a level of consciousness which as in alchemy can be attained not by force or by deceit, but through practice, trial and error, dedication, maturity and sincere efforts. The sun and the light, i.e. rationality, in real life destroy any attempt to integrate opposites. Those who try to possess this gift by force, i.e. to achieve this mental level of consciousness, will be punished by Nature itself. For example one of the robbers is killed by his partners and Encolpio realizes he has sinned and is punished by Priapus, one of the manifestations (or the son) of Hermes/Mercury the phallic god who makes his penis "wooden or dough like" (*di legno o di pasta*). Encolpio, by stealing the Hermaphrodite, and killing him/her, is punished by one of the negative manifestations of Hermes, impotence. He "lost his sword", "half crippled" in his impotent attempt to copulate he is teased as a "wet mouse on top of a fat slob" (*sorcio bagnato sopra una vacca*).

As Lopez-Pedraza points out, in *Giulietta degli spiriti*, Fellini portrays this concretized conjunction of opposites in the hermaphrodite in a scene in which he introduces a woman psychotherapist who has a manly body and stereotyped ideas about group therapy which she delivers in a gruff voice with a strong Northern European accent. This image, captured through Fellini's eyes, prompts the viewer to try to figure out just exactly how healing is procured at this level. She delivers healing precisely through the freakishness of her body – the concretized manifestation of the opposites, of the hermaphrodite – because it is impossible to imagine that any healing could come from the boring, horrifying jargon she spouts, a mixed salad of female pseudo-psychology (Lopez-Pedraza, 2003, p. 198).

Subversion of the Institution of the Family

Fellini's filmography is often characterized as criticism of patriarchal religious and secular authority, or any powerful group that uses emotionally laden symbols, social class, wealth, pleasure or attempts to hyperextend our abilities to compete aggressively, to work feverishly, to feel intensely and to think deliberately.

Fellini often assails the institution of the family and gender roles in marriage, and the well ordered family.

For instance, the plot of *Agenzia matrimoniale* focuses mostly on two themes, the search for the matrimonial agency, located inside a labyrinth of corridors, in an apartment building and the meeting, arranged by the agency, between the protagonist who is pretending to look for a spouse for his rich friend and a nice, simple poor woman. Just why the hero came to this agency remains unclear. Is he looking for a spouse for himself, or is he just pretending he wants to get married? Or, as a reporter is he going to make a scoop? The friend's disease is also uncommon: he is a lycanthrope, a werewolf, a person who transforms himself into a wolf during the night, a person who howls at the moon. Nevertheless the woman is ready to meet him and believes that she can deal with him.

The pretender at this point gives up and terminates his relationship with the woman. This can be seen as a turn of events, a stage trick, a *coup de theatre* which leaves the audience without closure. Was it a joke or a prank? Was the pretender acting in the name of a real friend? Was he really insane? Is lycanthropy a myth or a real disease? I am convinced that this plot challenges the basic meaning of marriage and the family. Lycanthropy is subversive in itself. It has to do with the night, the moon, and a person possessed by animal forces, or who imagines himself to be possessed. This short movie can be seen as an introduction to themes Fellini developed throughout his career.

Another example of criticism of the institution of the family can be found in the *White Sheik* whose plot deals with the honeymoon of a middle class young couple in Rome, the Eternal City. It starts, like other movies, and Fellini's own personal journey, with the couple's arrival at *Stazione Termini* in Rome. From the very beginning the husband dominates the situation, and orchestrates the accurate and obsessive planning of their vacation like a commander in chief. His inflated persona prompts him to follow rules, manners, and ridiculous bourgeois decorum "without a minute to spare". The husband is a typical petit-bourgeois product of the Italian provinces, characterized by his obsession with time and order, physical fastidiousness, and complete subservience to conventional morality. He is the antithesis of spontaneity and emotions,

> in the privacy of his new wife's company, his mask imposes a stern authoritarianism and an overbearing obsession with her respectability and purity. His worst fear is that his life will spin out of control, particularly as a result of some minor infraction of his strict moral code by his new wife, causing him a loss of face. (Bondanella, 1992, p. 82)

But the woman, subjugated by her obsessive husband, is very immature, and still in the thrall of romantic illusions. Her childish behavior upsets her husband's program and she spontaneously runs away to meet her photo-romance hero, the white sheik. She transgresses the norms of rationality of the well ordered family, and while pretending to take a bath she leaves the bathtub running in the hotel. She runs away, and mesmerized, enters the alluring world of fantasy: "her momentary truancy turns out to last an entire day and to be filled with misadventures for both of the newlyweds" (ibid, p. 83).The unconscious is related to photo-romance stories. One of the secretaries of the magazine tells her that "real life is that of the dream". The unconscious is also the countryside outside Rome, in the seaside town of Fregene, where she follows the photo-romance team who are taking new pictures. Here there is no sign of civilization, "without railway stations and without phones". She is overwhelmed by strong attraction and emotion, which are metaphorically depicted by the flood in the bathroom and the escape into the unconscious far away from the civilized city.

When she sneaks out to meet her photo-romance hero it takes her to the magazine's editorial office located on Via XXIV Maggio (May 24th Street) in

Rome. This street commemorates the day Italy entered the First World War. Symbolically the spouse decides to terminate a peaceful, false and boring honeymoon and begins an adventure which will trigger an inner war in her psyche and clashes in her conjugal relationship.

She escapes into a playful childish world, nicknaming herself "passionate dolly" and meeting her masked hero, *in vivo*, riding a seesaw in Fregene.

Their romantic boat trip suffuses the woman with strange happiness. Her suitor, the white sheik exclaims: "it is happiness which wells up from the memory of a posterior… anterior life… anterior? (sic), when who knows who we were, maybe I was a pirate and I am sure you were a mermaid" (my translation). She exclaims:" I am so happy, I am crazy and happy". But soon she realizes that her hero is married and an ordinary man, a vulgar suitor who is trying to seduce her. She is then insulted by his wife, teased by other actors, and finally has to admit that "her life is that of a dream, but a dream is also a fatal chasm". When she emerges from the bewitchment of her dream she pathetically tries to commit suicide and is hospitalized.

This is a kind of transformation from enchantment to death, which takes the heroine back to reality after her fugue into her childish fantasy, and after her attempt to violate the moral boundaries and her subjugated state of newlywed wife (Picchietti, 2002).

At the same time this truancy is exactly the opposite of what happens to her husband, who chases after her in a desperate attempt to protect the respectability of his social mask. He goes to the police who think he is deranged, and are ready to have him committed. He has to escape from the police and walk the streets of Rome during the night where he encounters the denizens of this dark world, the shadow which he tried to suppress behind his petty bourgeois mask of respectability, which includes among other things, two prostitutes (including protagonist of Cabiria) and a fire-eater. He is soothed by the warm and human presence of the prostitutes, and spends some time with one of them: "breaking his conventional code of ethics and destroying whatever claim he might earlier have had to bourgeois respectability" (Bondanella, 1992, p. 87).

We will never know if wife and husband engaged in any sexual infidelity during this time. But whatever happened, they are both shocked by the fact that beside the Catholic and *medio-borghese* decorum and the monogamous role of the family, other attractive and fearful worlds actually exist. As Bondanella points out:

> Both Wanda and Ivan are trapped in their respective roles. Wanda has tried to create a momentary realization of her empty romantic illusions, hoping to evade her social role as the faithful wife, but her attempts prove more and more unsatisfying. Ivan, on the other hand, works desperately to protect the respectability his social mask provides him, but he is equally hard pressed to maintain his performance. Neither of the two characters is really aware of the comedy of errors Fellini's narrative presents to the spectator, since their role-playing lacks even the slightest bit of self-consciousness. While we laugh at their mishaps, the other characters in the film begin to consider both of them mad. (1992, p. 86)

In the final scenes the two threads of the narrative are rejoined, signifying the ephemeral re-establishment of order, or at least a truce after their "first war", when both, escorted by his family, join a group of other young spouses on their honeymoon to attend a papal audience. The husband stresses that he does not want to know anything and that "the honor of the family comes first". In his way Fellini proclaims his "horror at the words of order by which we explain reality" (Free, 1973, p. 214).

We do not know whether the protagonists remain unchanged, or whether any dramatic epiphany will reflect a modification of their basic nature. The wife has to recognize the reality principle and give up her immature fantasies. The husband has to recognize that behind his mask of respectability, he possesses negative aspects that he denied in his life, the archetypal *shadow*. It is plausible that similar to "the traditional comic types they are, they remain essentially mechanical figures... trapped in their comic forms" (Bondanella, 1992, p. 89). Alternatively, from a more pessimistic feminist view, the wife may once again submit to patriarchal (papal) forces:

> Wanda's reintegration into a euphoric narrative is finally complete, however, when she transfers her fantasy from Fatima (the heroine of the photo-romance) into her wifely role, from the White Sheik to Ivan (her husband), and walks off blissfully to see the pope, the symbolic patriarch of Wanda's socially proper performance. (Picchietti, 2002, p. 102)

Having discovered unconscious parts of themselves, and the shadowy sides of the life (truancy, betrayal, infidelity, prostitution, suicide and insanity), having faced human aggression and been subverted by hypocritical reality, one message is that all these actions could perhaps endow them with a more integrated personality, which can combine the opposites of life.

IDIOCY AND MADNESS

The primitiveness of fools is usually much closer to that of the wild man, an imaginary remnant of a state in which man and Nature were one. The fool who nonsensically plays in the present may at the same time remind us of a past that precedes all of us, fools and non- fools alike, and that remains important to us. Fools are said to be silly, yet sometimes they are wise, like the high priests and even the gods. Like simpletons and the insane they are startled by new thoughts they discover every fleeting moment, they are sages and oracles, interpreting the ancient dramas and making a connection between present members of the tribe and their primeval ancestors (Willeford, 1969, p. 72).

Fools are characteristically unperturbed by the ignominy that comes with being irresponsible. They have a magical affinity with chaos that might allow them to serve as scapegoats on behalf of order, yet they elude the sacrifice or the banishment that would affirm order at their expense. They reduce order to chaos in a way that makes a farce of the mythical pattern (Willeford, 1969, p. 101). The figure of the idiot and fool, which has similarities with the clown, makes the concepts of trickster, freak and grotesque much clearer.

The theme of insanity, in particular lunacy, was the lynchpin of Fellini's final work *The voice of the moon,* where the fantastic, uncanny, the surreal, the verisimilar plot of a narrative thread woven into another story, and the distinction between insanity and real world collapses. The moon, instead of possessing lunatics, is captured in a peasant's net, a spectacle broadcast on-line. The Luna of the lunatics, as well as the Moon in Tarot cards stands for the goddess of the depths and a witch who opens the floodgates of dreams, intuitions, visions, ecstatic inspirations, mysticism and divination, but also releases fears, nightmares and madness from the dark world. Luna has immense power and therefore is dangerous. She can possess and destroy. This makes it crucial to confine this diffuse creativity to frameworks that can elicit creativity. In Tarot cards, the columns on both sides of the picture are boundaries and protection against emotional power. These are the male columns that support the Moon's feminine ambiguous power (Netzer, 2008, p. 77).

The etymological root of both moon and mind is the Indo-European manas, mana, or men, representing the Great Mother's wise blood in women, governed by the moon. Its derivative 'mania' originally meant ecstatic revelation, just as lunacy used to mean possession by the spirit of Luna, the moon. To be moon touched, or moon struck meant to be chosen by the

Goddess; a moon calf was one carried away by love. When patriarchal thinkers belittled the Goddess, these words came to mean mere craziness (Walker, 1983, p. 669-670).

The fool or the lunatic usually survives both his clumsiness and stupidity, yet his final survival seems a triumph not so much of the human will as of something else. The functioning of the fool's will is often an expression of his derangement. Very often in human dealings with the supernatural, the breakdown of form is taken to imply possession by a higher power; something of this view continues to live on in our attitude toward protagonists who are fools.

In one of the first dreams reported by Fellini, il Pazzo, the fool, saves his life from falling off a roof (February 12, 1961).The figure of Gelsomina in *La strada* may have a kernel of ambivalence toward the primary figure of the woman. On the one hand she is like a male clown, a bit strange, not like other girls. She is too naïve, simple and pure, and is probably retarded or dim-witted. But her relatedness to the earth, children, the handicapped, animals and inanimate objects is unique such that she is something of an "idiot-savant",

> she has a strange affinity with nature and seems most at home by the seashore.... Gelsomina walks by a solitary tree and imitates with her arms the angle of its only branch. Immediately afterward, she listens enraptured to the almost musical sound of the telegraph wires that only she seems capable of hearing. (Bondanella, 1992, p. 104)

In one way Gelsomina did not develop in her culture, but rather has a primitive and feminine gift of mystical communion, a *participation mystique* in that she is capable of merging with the voices of the nature, has intuitions and is attuned to forces that modern culture has lost. Gelsomina in *La strada* soon leaves Zampanò behind as she grows in understanding and love, while he remains unchanged by the experience of the road, living on an exclusively physical level, satisfying his appetites of food, sex and sleep with little regard for the niceties of civilized society. The change in Gelsomina is elicited by the Fool, *Il Matto* (as a sign of archetype he has no name) who impersonates Zampanò's disembodied, ethereal male opposite (Marcus, 1993, pp. 92-93). The fool in "the very embodiment of his mental agility accords to Gelsomina, for his figurative language bears constant witness to his own associational powers...he teaches Gelsomina to think abstractly, to transcend the limits of the material world" (Marcus, 1993, p. 95). Also because of his subversive character, and his capacity to tell the truth and challenge Zampanò's masculine vulgarity, he will be killed by him.

CLOWNS

Clowns have many of the facets of idiots and fools. Clowning is a convenient, and hence recurring, means of vitalizing awareness of both the universal and the particular by ensuring that they are kept together. Clowns condense humor by drawing on sex and obscenity based on sickness, sorrow, misfortune and mockery of foreigners (Willeford, 1969, p. 83). Circus clowns playfully give birth and playfully kill. Clowns provoke and play in accordance with specific cultural attitudes and in violation of others and pursue a shifting compromise between allegiance and rebellion. They question the adequacy of cultural attitudes by reminding us of these ambiguities and by adopting other attitudes, thus implying that those of the audience are arbitrary. Clowns are semidetached from social authority: what they do is a mixture of the anti-cultural and of play: they produce in their audience what could be called a suspension of belief or of value (Willeford, 1969, p. 96).

Fellini, when discussing his film *I Clowns*, said: "the clown was always the caricature of a well-established, ordered, peaceful society. But today all is temporary, disordered and grotesque. Who can still laugh at clowns? Hippies, politicians, the man in the street, all the world plays the clown, now" (quoted in Free, 1973, p. 214). Like fools, clowns can also trigger a suspension of disbelief and devaluation, which becomes an avenue of exploration towards a self-authenticating spiritual power. This is because the jester's power to speak the truth, even when his master cannot, was based on the convention that, for him, everything, including the most sacred matters, was mere play (Willeford, 1969, pp. 97-98).

The following dream dated December 20, 1966, captures the positive force of Fellini's inner clown, so well expressed in his movie, *I Clowns*:

> Scardamaglia shows me a document from his company in which, among other projects, there is a program of Fellini films in the center of the page. The program will be produced by a company named "Jolly" (note [by Fellini]: Jolly is the Italian joker, the card that can resolve any combination because it has a variable, adaptable value, the value you assign in any given hand) (2008, p. 505).

In Fellini's movies, the clown functions as the rebel, who highlights the deficiencies of his time (Free, 1973, p. 226). Obsessed by seriousness and intellectualizing, we forget that the grotesque and the absurd can be a joy as well a terror. If our culture is breaking down, it might be because we have forgotten how to laugh at ourselves. Such laughter is Fellini's strength (Free, 1973, p. 227). As stressed, for many reason Fellini becomes the clown himself, subverting the order of our real world.

FREAKS

A freak situation is one in which there is a sudden and apparently inexplicable change or turn of events. It can refer to the mind, an abnormal product or a curious unusual object, anomaly or aberration. It can also be a person or animal on exhibition such as some strange deviation from nature including a monster, anything unusual odd or irregular, an action that becomes uninhibited, excited or deranged; it can refer to a loss one's sanity, composure, or mental stability.

Besides stories of clowns and fools, the quintessential freak situation can be seen in Fellini's Satyricon that involves images of the god Priapus, the son of Hermes (sometimes in Greek mythology, Hermes himself) (Lopez-Pedraza, 2003, p. 194). In fact, both the film and the book Satyricon show the ups and downs in the sexual rivalry between Encolpio and Ascilto over the possession the young slave Giton. There is a constant longing for potency, which in fact reveals impotence and weakness (Lopez-Pedraza, 2003, p. 194). This is the stage cue for Priapus, one of the sexual derivatives of Hermes, the god of erection and its opposite, impotence.

In medicine, there is a well-known illness which takes its name from Priapus-Priapism. This rare illness manifests itself in men, who supposedly have had a very vigorous sexual life. This illness turns vigorous sexuality into what physicians call an impotent erection. These extremes of potency and irreparable weakness were also typical of Fellini's *Casanova.*

Sarcastic laughs, groans, mutual bitchery, use of nicknames, raspberries, sexual allusions, vernacular language, farts, etc. also challenge the adult, old fashioned and traditional generation. These can be seen as freak behaviors that are found in most of Fellini's movies. Oddities, sticking out the tongue, chatterboxes, wry faces and grimaces, foolish faces, coquettish women belching and farting are all leitmotifs in Fellini that have their own long vulgar vernacular literary history (see the Canterbury Tales). For instance, Fellini's banquet reaches its climax in an endless luncheon of bad taste in the Trimalchio's house in the Satyricon. Even the director, while supervising the shot of the scenes, joins the actors and throws food (as shot in Gideon

Bachman's documentary). This is a world of flesh and sensuality, spiced by gossip, esthetic attempts at poetry, vulgar dancing and orgiastic music.

Another freak scene can be found in Amarcord, when uncle Teo, a madman at the top of a tree, shouts for hours that he needs a woman (again telling the truth) and is completely oblivious to any attempts to get him down. Finally he is easily subdued by a tiny, dwarf-like, freakish nun. He didn't mean that woman…

The connection between the possible healing qualities of the female therapist in Giulietta and the rather freakish little nun who can subdue a madman simply by her presence is that both are part of the archetypal appearance of the freak (Lopez-Pedraza, 2003, p. 198). Fellini's special gift for rendering freakish images is breathtaking in particular in his *Casanova.* A good example is the theatrical performance by their host dressed in a gorgeous turquoise blue gown with little butterfly wings, personifying Psyche and a beautiful boy, personifying Eros (also known as Cupid). The central feature is Eros' huge tongue constantly flicking in and out of Psyche's mouth. Fellini also exploited other small facial movements to give an animal-like sense of freakishness. A dream dated December 13, 1974, portrays N. a woman completely naked "who eats with animal-like voraciousness". Elsewhere in his Intervista Fellini mentions that movement of the nostrils makes a woman's face seem horsy and more sensually animal like. Freakish characters continue to be found in Fellini's late works. For example a there is a parade of freaks in Ginger and Fred when they appear in a commercial TV program:

> …a transvestite who claims that her vocation is to bring love [that is, sex] to the inmates of Italian prisons; an engineer who holds the record for the longest time spent in captivity by kidnappers and the highest ransom paid, whose finger was cut off and sent to his relatives during the negotiations with his captors; a woman who abandons her family because she falls in love with an extraterrestrial. Then there is a man who can impregnate a woman simply by his glance, the maker of edible underwear, a Mafioso complete with police escorts, a cow with fifteen teats, and last but not least, twenty-five dwarf dancers called 'Los Lilliputs'. (Bondanella, 1992, p. 224)

This movie reminds a Hermetic claim against mass communication of the "Big Brother". It reveals cover-ups of the political and economical Italian system, persisting in "speaking out more or less candidly about what he sees, right alongside the Zeus establishment and its Apollonian allies (scientific and military technology). (Paris, 1990, p. 80)

The presence of freak figures, hoodlums, loafers etc. is depicted in one of the first dreams reported by Fellini, dated February, 6, 1961.These images are reminiscent of the opening scenes of the first night of *I vitelloni*:

> Amid nasty laughter, jokes and shrill whistles a small group of late-night revelers (many of whom are pederasts), drag a long fireman's ladder from one big building door to another among the little piazzas and alleyways of ancient Rome. Here's someone clinging up there at the top. They knock on the big doors, windows are thrown open, and the hoodlums as if they were looking for the home of that guy up there at the top of the ladder... giggles, Bronx cheers, the ladder is pushed towards another door with a great clamor of wheels over the old pavement. Guidarino, a fat buffoon, explains what's happening to me with tears of laughter in his eyes, producing a radio commentator's report of his weird game he finds so extraordinarily silly. The long ladder sways, trembles. What if I was that guy clinging up there? We know almost nothing about him and now that I'm writing down this dream I think that he's definitely me, an empty soulless shell who doesn't think, suffer, feel, or sense anything. He seems a great deal like me, in the end he swings back and forth in the night's darkness, as light as a ghost. (2008, p. 473)

Mages

Throughout human history certain fools have been clairvoyants or mediums: their divine or demonic inspiration is a special instance of the fool's ability to speak the truth, or be a sage in fool's clothing. But even more characteristic of fools and folly is precisely that their truth telling is not necessarily central, that it is more or less interchangeable with expressions of stupidity, madness and freakishness. According to Willeford, this attitude leads to confusion between what has value (sanity or truth of whatever kind) and what has none (insanity or nonsense): it is this confusion that is central; i.e., the fact that diamonds and dull stones are treated as interchangeable, and that both of them are either supremely valuable or worthless depending upon the momentary state of the fool's mind. Many fools represent an *abaissement du niveau mental* – a loosening of a hold on consciousness that allows unconscious content and modes of behavior to usurp the place of conscious awareness and thus provides meaningful insights (Willeford, 1969, p. 80). Many of these processes are magic.

The magician is the first card in Tarot, and its picture is somewhat reminiscent of the first letter in the Hebrew alphabet, with one hand raised upward toward the sky and one hand toward the ground: the aleph- א. From a low mental level in his left hand, he can connected to the spiritual sky. The mage in Tarot is also the shaman, and the alchemist son of Hermes. It brings about changes in people's minds that affect their inner development. In Tarot, the magician represents the connection between the manifest and the secret, the conscious and the unconscious. Its knowledge is infinite channeled into finite man (Netzer, 2008, p. 44-45).

According to Jung, the wise old man appears in dreams in the guise of a doctor, priest, teacher, professor, grandfather or any other person possessing authority, but also in the guise of a magician. Perhaps the best example of Fellini's use of the mage figure is the magician Maurice who is teamed with the telepathic Maya in *8 ½*.The mage also appears as the hermaphrodite guru Bishma, who speaks in tongues with peculiar accents and uses free association. Bishma, apparently a teacher of Buddhism, is in fact a hermaphrodite, and hence sexually complicated, but also a medium through whom spirits may speak. He knows the secret of love of both sexes as shown in his meeting with the female protagonist in *Giulietta degli spiriti*.

The magician's energy is the archetype of awareness and insight, but he also possesses knowledge of everything that is not immediately apparent and commonsensical (Moore and Gillette, 1991, p. 106). He is an initiator into the secrets of hidden knowledge of all kinds. The mage has the power of telepathy (in *81/2*), he can lead a séance, deflate arrogance ("you are a derelict"), and see through denial and exercise discernment *(Giulietta degli spiriti*). For example, once the séance with a medium begins, the impact on Giulietta is dramatic. She has visions of castles, dark forests, streets, and faces with sparkling eyes that she had when she was a girl but had since lost. She discovers that the spirits want to contact her again.

The mage is also the catalyst of future tragedies as portrayed in *Le notti di Cabiria*, when the heroine, the fragile prostitute, under hypnosis by a vaudeville mage, is forced to disclose her unconscious weakness, her craving for love in the presence of a theater audience. Soon afterwards she is seduced by one of the spectators who takes advantage of this intimate information disclosed under hypnosis.

TRICKSTERS

In mythology, certain gods can also be thieves. The image of this firsttheft, when Hermes robbed his brother Apollo, may suggest that there is a temptation to rob someone who is close to us: in this particular myth the theft takes place, shamelessly, within the kinship of brotherhood (Lopez-Pedraza, 2003, p. 58). As Kerenyi points out (1990, p. 52): "despite the thievery and deceit and shamelessness – and this is probably the most wonderful thing about it – a divine innocence is properly suited to and inherent in it. Hermes has nothing to do with sins and atonement. What he brings with him from the springs of creation is precisely the innocence of becoming".

In Fellini's *Swindle* (*Il bidone*) small-time crooks impersonate priests and civil servants to con poor people out of their money. They also con their families. For example Carlo, one of the gang, says to his wife that he is a salesman, with ambitions to become a painter. The members of the gang believe that the world is full of idiots, but the victims in general are poor people. Augusto, the elder trickster, is attracted to criminals who are brilliant, clever and accomplished, who take risks and succeed. However Augusto also harbors an inner conflict, and despite his age, seems redeemable, in particular when he meets his religious and righteous daughter, his lost inner anima, and realizes he should take on the duties of an adult ("today young people work for a living" she says). In the final scene, when he claims that he has a heart, his friend teases him that this is a novel, and when he pretends he was not able to swindle an invalid girl and a poor family, his incredulous partners call his trick (to deceive them) as "the dumbest trick of his life". In fact, it was his last swindle (although the audience believes that he is speaking the truth, thus redeeming himself, in extremis). This act will cost him his life.

Chapter 4

The Eternal Child (Puer Aeternus)

Youthfulness is also characteristic of Hermes. His youthful image was the only classical-Hellenistic form that was suitable for both the divine child and the son (Kerenyi, 1990, p. 83). Hermes is connected to the archetype of the Child in general and the Eternal Child in particular, an anti-hero who seeks opportunities, and cannot be committed to anything or to anybody. Many figures in Fellini's work, like Augusto, the protagonist in *Swindle*, act under Hermes' influence by maintaining childish patterns. Augusto cannot wait to grow up and try new things, convinced that "the grass is greener on the other side". He is always restless. As Shinoda Bolen (1989) noted, the child in Hermes' character usually starts out well; he is charming, friendly and makes a good impression on others. However he is unable to stick to a job or an idea.

Augusto may think that he is immortal and that he has all the time he needs, until it is too late. While other more mature people are building up their own careers and family, he is still looking for adventure. One day he discovers that his life has passed him by and that he is getting old, that there is no escape and no final redemption. In his attempt to go out with a bang and settle the score with his comrades, he is accidentally killed by them.

It is interesting to note that Fellini rarely dealt with children as protagonists (with the exception of *Amarcord*). In a few scenes they are cripples (*La strada, Il bidone*), or they are more mature than adults. Sometimes they work (Augusto's daughter in *Il bidone*, the little boy, Moraldo's friend in *I vitelloni* and the beautiful bartender girl in *La dolce vita*). Sometimes they live higher spiritual experiences such as miraculous mystic visions in *La dolce vita*. The biological order is therefore subverted. Children are mature, whereas grown up adults remain eternal, immature, and child-like, like Titta's vulgar grandfather in *Amarcord.*

The epithet *vitellone* that combines the Italian words for beef and veal, means an immature, lazy adult person devoid of a clear identity or any notion of what to do in life. The title of the movie *I vitelloni* is the perfect description of the five listless young males from the sleepy Italian provinces, whose actions, or rather inactions, constitute a type of social condition (Bondanella, 1992, p. 90). They are and remain eternal children. As Baranski points out (1993, p. 73-76) a state of *vitellone* is a freaky condition of immaturity characterized by two attitudes.

The first is an inability to accept the responsibilities brought about by a preference for the world of dreams, a refusal of social responsibility, in particular in work and the family (scorn for conventional forms of employment, closely coupled to a parasitic relationship with their breadwinning families). The eternal child of Hermes can be very charming and convincing while he courts a girl. But he does not want commitment (in particular when she gets pregnant).This is the case for example for Fausto in *I vitelloni*, who tries to run away when he finds out that his girlfriend Sandra is pregnant. Because of his irresponsible behavior he is finally whipped by his father like the child he is and will always remain before a reconciliation takes place with Sandra that will most likely not last very long.

Second, the eternal child merges into the group but is unable to create a strong and independent personality:

> As long as he is cocooned by the group, then the *vitellone* is safe. The group's behavior and particularly its conversation, which consists either of banalities or impossible musings centered on pranks, sex, wealth, and adventure, bear little relation to the real world, thus bolstering the individual's belief that what he is doing is, in fact, the norm. (Baranski, 1993, pp. 75-76)

In general, the man who is identified with this archetype of the Eternal Child (*Puer Aeternus*) remains an adolescent too long; that is, the traits that are normal in a seventeen or eighteen year old extend into later life, coupled in most cases with over-dependence on the mother (von Franz, 2000). Most of the Puer characteristics untidiness, exhibitionism, forgetfulness and tardiness, not keeping to schedule, could come under the psychological heading of a "weak ego" (Paris, 1990, p.110). In terms of pathology, the Eternal Child appears as a specific style of prolonged adolescence, a moratorium in Eriksonian vocabulary, a condition of mental stagnation sometimes ending with sudden violent death (Hillman, 2005, p. 187). Fellini's *Toby Dammit* is a good example.

Jung states that in cases of eternal children, there is a fear of life:

> the young, growing part of the personality, if prevented from living or kept in check, generates fear and changes into fear. The fear seems to come from the mother, but actually it is the deadly fear of the instinctive, unconscious, inner man who is cut off from life by the continual shrinking back from reality. If the mother is felt as the obstacle, she then becomes the vengeful pursuer. Naturally it is not the real mother, although she too may seriously injure her child by the morbid tenderness with which she pursues it into adult life, thus prolonging the infantile attitude beyond the proper time. (Jung, 1957, vol. 5, p. 298)

The eternal child is characterized by his inability to begin the journey of the hero: the hero is psychologically that function within the ego that has the capacity and the courage to face the frightening unknown in a conscious search for meaning (Logos) and relatedness (Eros). The hero abandons the known and the typical, the normative and the mediocre, often without knowing what lies ahead, yet is the only one who attends the call (Shalit, 2008, p. 58). He breaks away from the bonds of the mother, and does not follow in the father's footsteps. The hero turns away from his father's house, away from his country, away from his safety. Where there is soul, the ego is required to abandon its lazy comfortable existence in mass-man's conformist consciousness, the confines of conventions and collective consciousness of the crowd (Shalit, 2008, p.59).

The eternal child as an anti-hero is unable to enter time or to grow old, and presents a curious antiquarianism of self-destructiveness, imbued with a desire to fail, to fall, or some sort of amorality. He is still living and exploiting an exaggerated parental constellation. The eternal child is that structure of consciousness and pattern of behavior that refuses and struggles with the mature wise person – time, work, order, limits, learning, history, continuity survival and endurance – that is driven by a sane libido to inquire, seek, travel, pursue, search to transgress all limits. It is a restless spirit that has no "home" on earth, is always coming from somewhere or going to somewhere in transition (Hillman, 2005, p. 187-188).

The mammas' boys, the Italian *vitelloni* or *mammoni* or sometimes the papas' boys, the Italian *figli di papà,* are the perennial adolescent. They are not only the early anti-heroes in *La dolce vita, I vitelloni, 8½* like Snaporaz, Marcello, Guido and Augusto, but also later versions of aged pathetic anti-heroes like Pippo in *Ginger and Fred* or Snaporaz again in the *City of women.* In their experiences, there is a lack of progress and reality, and they show signs of weakness and helplessness at the beginning of any enterprise. The horizontal world, the space-time continuum we call reality that has to be conquered, is not their world. For example the *vitelloni*, with the one exception of Moraldo, who represents the surprise in the finale, cannot leave their city. They make fun of work. They move and act as a collective. They believe in fate. "Finding a job is a matter of days", they have all kinds of excuses to avoid work, and dream about impossible prestigious jobs, like screenplays for the theater. They are self-absorbed by their vanity and appearance, stuck in their static immobility: mustaches, sideburns and pointed beards ("the biggest event this winter" according to the narrator). They want to stay up in the air and not touch the earth. In other words they have a creative problem, whereas their libido is stuck, and they lack pragmatism and mobility. They are in a state of boredom, which is a symptom of life dammed up like a river, where one does not know how to get what one has within oneself into reality. They have an expression on their faces as though they know all about life and feel very, very old (von Franz, 2000, p. 66-67). But they live at home, cannot leave the comfortable nest, and exploit the family (parents and working sisters). However, they get upset when they are criticized for their immaturity. Fausto exclaims: “I am treated like a 5 year old, but I am 30!”

When watching *I vitelloni*, or meeting Snaporaz in two different period of his life (*8½* and *City of women*) as well as other male heroes in Fellini's work (Augusto, Checco, Peppo, and the protagonist of the *White sheik* interpreted by Alberto Sordi), there is a strange attitude or feeling that they are not yet in real life. For the time being these individuals are doing this or that, but whether it is a woman or a job, it is not yet what they really want, and there is a fantasy that sometime in the future the real thing will come about. If this attitude is prolonged, it means a constant inner refusal to commit oneself to the moment, to what is there in the here and now. There is always the fear of being caught in a situation from which it may be impossible to slip out again (working and getting married, the Freudian "work and love"). They generally do not like activities which require patience and long training; they do not want to be burdened by any kind of weight. The one thing they absolutely refuse is responsibility for anything, or to carry the weight of a situation (von Franz, 2000, p. 9).

Augusto, the "biggest con man" in the movie *Il bidone* is 48 years old, and is a pathetic figure who cannot develop and change his pattern of behavior: the older he gets, the more he clings to the illusion that one day he will do *it.*

Augusto and his partners are attracted by the glamour of the Italian post-war nouveau riches with their cars, women and houses. He is attracted by jokes, pranks and immediate bodily satisfactions. He just wants to "pass the time" (*tirare avanti*). Because of his childish attitude he cannot develop into a mature adult, work normally or be involved in the education of his daughter. His partners have grandiose dreams to become singers and writers, but they remain "wimps" or "jerks" in their attempts to rob people.

The *vitelloni*, who tease workers, and blow a raspberry at them (as Fellini did as a youngster), dream about leaving town, going to Milan, Rome, Brazil or Africa, to enjoy "freedom-travel-parties." These are people who have no hold on earth, they fly off it; they are able to assimilate everything psychologically, but have great difficulty achieving things in reality. Unlike Fellini, who never defined himself as a *vitellone*, they never start the journey, first leaving their home, their town, moving to the Center, to the Capital, the Eternal City, or in psychological terms, developing their connections with the Self (integration or individuation in Jungian terms). They pass the time as hoodlums, creating havoc at night by playing student pranks. But they are somehow aware of their tragic condition. When Alberto sees the clowns in the Carnival, and then sees himself, he is half drunk but utters the truth: "you are nobodies!" Only Moraldo takes a step because he feels that he "must leave". It is clear that he has learned something from his experiences, in particular after he meets a young boy who worked for his living. But when he leaves on the train, we have no way of knowing whether his escape to Rome will have a maturing effect:

> Each of the three *vitelloni* experiences a crisis as his illusions collide with reality. Their lives move on the surface of reality, and when superficial responses to serious problems no longer suffice, they return to the soothing comfort of their womblike family shelters, outwardly pretending to their friends that nothing has changed, yet now privately conscious of the inadequacy of their damaged illusions. (Bondanella, 1992, p. 93)

The pathetic figure of a tricky, dishonest middle aged man, who may be impotent and will never become a rich and famous comedy actor (*capocomico*), is also personified by De Filippo in signor Checco in *Luci del varietà* (*Variety Lights*, 1950). He is also suggestive of the character of Pippo in *Ginger and Fred*, who is possessed by a faulty self, a distorted persona. Both still have grandiose dreams: "All artistic Italy will notice our successes", signor Checco says, but in fact, they are penniless little men, with criminal records, teased by their colleagues and the public, unable to establish a relationship with the only woman who really loves them. Pippo, in his pathetic live dance performance, falls down during a live broadcast. He was never a great dancer, and his performance as a drunk, penniless geezer is a pathetic part of a parade of other freakish people.

THE WOMB AND THE ETERNAL CHILD

Images of the symbolic womb, the tunnel, the grotto and the cave appear in Fellini's work, and can also be related to the condition of the eternal child captured by negative aspects of the womb of the Great Mother (this theme will be developed in the last chapter). According to Van Watson, one the most famous imageries in all of Fellini's filmography, the opening of *8½*, begins with a sequence of the suffocating Guido (Fellini's alter-ego) "enwombed *in* his car *in* a traffic jam *in* a tunnel. Guido momentarily assumes the fetal position as he climbs out of his car, furthering the gestational metaphor" (2002, pp. 85-86, his italics). As the story line continues, Guido cannot develop a mature sexual relationship and intimate commitment, and cannot express his inner creativity as a movie director. He remains in a liminal state, supposedly cured by thermal water in a spa. However, Van Watson fails to recognize that the final scene has a similar sequence of suffocation, when Guido is unable to escape from the many photographers and reporters ambushing him and re-assumes the fetal position under a table. This *finale* shows that the protagonist cannot liberate himself from his fixation on the womb and cannot develop into a mature person capable of coping with the principles of reality, making decisions and assuming responsibility in career and his marital life. In a circular regressive movement the final scene returns to the point of departure. This is a typical uroboric movement, without development and growth. Guido remains a child and withdraws into infancy. Ouroboros (or Uroboros) is Greek for the Hermetic World Serpent, sometimes the Sea-serpent Oceanus encircling the earth, sometimes the underground python coiled in the earth's womb (Walker, 1983, p. 754). In a significant hypnagogic experience Fellini writes (November, 5 1976): "In the dark, dirty air I can't manage to fly away and rack the starry sky because I'm tied to a big black sea serpent that is tenaciously, indissolubly bound to me and the dark, scary sea".

In Jungian terms, this figure is not developed and is typical of the pre-ego dawn state. Being or returning into the womb, despite its protection and nurturing functions, can be a form of imprisonment, burial and regression. It is no accident that Guido, in this final sequence, commits or attempt to commit suicide in a fetal, ouroboric position. However being in the womb also has the potential of a new birth, and new forms of creation. The anti-hero of *8½* finds no solution.

Conti is a more optimistic in her analysis of the finale:

> Transfigured by the creative act, join hands in a round carousel, a living mandala signifying the birth of the whole man, and the reunion of the ego and the self. In fact, Guido too, abandoning with the megaphone his role of director and holding the hand of Luisa, joins the circle. The individuation process is thus completed. From it, a child is born, as only the little Guido remains dancing in a circle of light at the end of the day. This child, another symbol of the rejuvenated self, is the bearer of new hopes that will light the way to the man who has finally accepted his maturity (1972, p. 161).

It is more plausible in terms of Fellini's personal acceptance of life to see this as a "celebration of the triumph of Fellini's own artistic creativity", a sign of mild optimism more that a real step of maturation forward taken by the protagonist. Individuation in Jungian terms is a project of the entire life. It doesn't happen suddenly. Moreover, Fellini always tried to avoid completely logical conclusions and moral judgments in his films: "my films don't have what is called a final scene. The story never reaches its conclusion" (cited in Bondanella, 1992, p. 95). As I would argue, Fellini's heroes never reach individuation or complete their living mandala. Thus this finale is not a reality, but is beyond reality, a hopeful fantasy which is detached from the trajectory of the plot. It is a meta-cinematic reference typical of Fellini's style (Bondanella, 1992, p. 178). Following Kezich this scene can be seen as the stoic, playful acceptance of life's assault (2006, p. 243).

This final scene can also be interpreted as a form of hope, but not for Guido, an eternal child who throughout the movie makes no steps toward progress or to become more mature and reach an integrative inner individuation. If Guido is transformed it is only by death. In the final scene, he creates a circus ring and leads a childish dance around the ring and out (the Italian *girotondo*), leaving only the uniformed child version of himself in the spotlight to exit into the darkness playing a piccolo.

This minimalistic form of hope is typical in Fellini's style. There is a similar kind of finale in Cabiria's story, after she confronts the risk of death for the second time and sees all her hopes dashed with the loss of all her savings, house included. In this moment of despair, she is accidentally escorted by a group of singers of Roman *stornelli* on the road. The victimized Cabiria is not transformed but is briefly encouraged to stay alive, knowing at least theoretically that there is a possibility of transformation in the future. At the end, her face fills the screen, a little smile once more in evidence (Alpert, 1986, p. 112). This is a sort of mild optimism, or a puckish Fellinian wink.

For many reasons most of Fellini's heroes do not develop into a new state of consciousness: there is no change in their state as eternal children, they are never deeply transformed or reborn. Even if they make fun of or comply with the collective consciousness, the safety of home, rules, roles and regulations, they are not ready to depart on their inner journey or prepare for their journey across the sea as real heroes.

Crossing the ocean in many cultures is a form of initiation, or a way of approaching the abyss of the unconscious. As portrayed in Fellini's dream dated November 12, 1961, jumping into the sea, swimming in the darkness in dangerous waves is a sign of bravery and a message to the dreamer that "we can move on". Crossing the sea is dangerous and the navigator has to take risks, in the center of a catastrophic typhoon because "jumping into the big wave of real life also means dying" (dream in October 3, 1961).

Fellini's protagonists do not cross the ocean. Their path, as in the *E la nave va* (*Ships sails on*), do not turn the passengers into heroes-to-be because the ship does not cross the sea to discover new continents, it just sinks into the ocean. The protagonists are stuck in their persona and do not embark on their own heroic adventure on the open sea, which symbolizes the depths of unconscious. The atmosphere of the *Ships sails on* is morbid and decadent as it follows the cult of a deceased opera diva. The ship sails on, but the passengers are not brought to a new state on an inner continent. In the movie there are two suggestions as to how this new state can be reached: the unusual vertical meeting between the sailors who work in the fire stokehold and the noble and decadent opera singers who perform for them, showing their ability to modulate their artistic voices inside the engine room. In this condition, hellish physical work encounters an unusual situation in the divine, sublimated artistic performance. This can be seen as a metaphor of the axis between layers of consciousness in human beings: the earth, close to fire, and the ethereal voice close to heaven; manual workers and opera singers.

The same metaphor holds for the informal meeting between the decadent Italian noble passengers and the presence of poor Serbian refugees packed on the deck of the ship. The dance on the deck is art, when high society respectability and manners are possessed by a primordial pagan sensual gypsy dance that bridges the ethnic and socio-economic gap. All dance together, having found a joyful and common language of solidarity, cutting the physical rope which divided classes.

Another suggestion as to how the static condition of eternal child can develop is also made on a metaphorical level. When the singers discuss the capacity of the deceased diva to produce uncanny sounds as part of her repertoire it is said that she visualized a seashell. Her voice spiraled up, "like a catalyst of energy". This spiral movement can be interpreted as a possible path not only for singers but for any human who wants to get rid of a static circular movement or a static horizontal uroboric condition, and develop into a spiral movement that leads to new states of personal growth and consciousness. The image of the awakening serpent or the Kundalini, in Indian mythology, illustrates this notion.

The movie *Toby Dammit* is a short illustration of the static condition of an eternal child who is attracted to death, and cannot develop his psyche and grow up. The protagonist is always drunk, and depicts himself as "a night person. I hate light."

He is possessed by feminine forces of the Devil. His hallucinations are about a young white female figure tempting him with a white ball. When asked whether the devil looks like a goat, a bat or a black cat, Toby answers, revealing the identity of hallucination of the young girl at the airport : "No... I'm English, not Catholic. To me the devil is cheerful, agile. He looks like a little girl".

Toby is an addict and LSD is way of achieving his normal state. He is narcissistic, whimsical and dislikes his public. He is violent, unpredictable and neurotic: "I am not a great actor. My last director complained because I was drunk. Wine makes me sad". Despite his childish labile character, he is awarded the She-Wolf (*Lupa*) prize in Rome.

The opposite positive female image is that of an erotic temptress in black, who is mature and friendly and who promises to stay with him forever. "A woman took my hand; she said 'I am here for you"'. This woman may represent positive and protective aspects of the Great Mother. But his death wish, to be devoured by the Terrible Mother, little white girl, is too strong.

He drives his new Ferrari, at night when he is drunk, in search of Rome, the Eternal City, and probably his inner mental center or balance. He drives through a labyrinth of dead end streets, fog and hellish landscapes. He has to take a detour, because a bridge is being built. He is tempted to drive off the bridge. He is looking for his inner center, but he dies in an accident beheaded. His head is collected by the diabolic white girl, representing the Devil or

Mother Death. A key feature in this film is the anti-hero's failure on his journey, who, when possessed by the unconscious, makes an ultimate attempt to kill the dragon with his Ferrari phallic weapon. In other words, running off the bridge, and trying to jump onto the other side may be seen as an attempt in extremis to reach a new state of consciousness, to free himself from his eternal state of childhood. The threshold is not only the boundary between outside and inside but also the possibility of passage from one zone to another. But it is especially the images of the bridge and the narrow gate which suggest the idea of a dangerous passage and which, for this reason, frequently occur in liminal states, in initiatory and funerary rituals and mythologies. Initiation, death, mystical ecstasy, absolute knowledge, all these are equivalent to passage from one mode of being to another and bring about a veritable ontological mutation. To suggest paradoxical passage (since passage always simplifies a break and a transcendence), various religious traditions have made plentiful use of the symbolism of the perilous bridge or the narrow gate.

In Fellini's *Casanova* the protagonist, despite his grandiose self-esteem, after having wandered all over Europe in search of a noble patron and benefactor ends his life as a lonely miserable librarian, mingling with vulgar servants, teased, and mocked: "I am a famous Italian writer, a literate man, a philosopher". But even his infantile whims ("I want my dish of macaroni!") are not fulfilled, and he is reduced to a tottering and sick carcass, bedecked with plumes and powdered like an old clown. For Fellini, Casanova was not an individual. He was absorbed by theatrical action "thinking according to a compulsory system of generic slogans without meaning [with] debased emotion at a physiological and feverish temperature – in short, adolescence in its most declining phase" (Fellini, 1978, p. 30).

Casanova is also an eternal child. In this case, according to the Jungian approach, the image of the mother- the image of the perfect woman - prompts the search for a mother goddess, so that each time he is fascinated by a woman only later to discover that she is an ordinary human being (von Franz, 2000, p. 7). Once he has been intimate with her, any woman, even old or a mechanical doll, the whole fascination vanishes and he turns away disappointed, only to project the image anew onto one woman after another. The doll will remain his last object of desire.

Freud used the term *Unheimlich* which literally means a condition of being homeless, in relation to inanimate objects that mimic reality, like dolls, marionettes or robots. These express simulacra that create a feeling of alienation prompted by the merging of the animate and the inanimate. This was the central trait of Fellini's *Casanova*.

There is something pathetic about the way Casanova, like the classic Don Juan tries in vain to connect to his soul. He seems to have a certain awareness of his damnation, and it is not until there are no other alternatives that at last he has the vague fantasy of finding a solution. The opening of the movie, with the emersion and immersion of the huge Venus (Venice) head, foreshadows the life of Fellini's Casanova as an anti-hero in his attempts to emerge from his life, and the possession of his unconscious, and simultaneously how he loses his way, and sinks back into the abyss. Unlike the real character, Fellini depicts a person who does not really live his life. He is an eternal child, a dreamer. Moreover he is grotesque, macabre and ghostly pale.

Eternal children are constantly in rehearsal, incapable of starting the real performance of life, or becoming heroes, performing their own music. Fellini's *Prova d'orchestra* (*Orchestra rehearsal*), can be seen as a metaphor of this pattern in the life. Their meeting- place is closed, like a womb, and under the floor there are ancient graves of popes. These living performers are therefore close to death inside mother earth.

The orchestra is:

> a completely chaotic group of comic characters… the conductor is a lonely, authoritarian figure, appropriately of German nationality. His relationship to his musicians is strained… he vituperates the musicians mercilessly… the musicians' revolt against the director is an obvious parody of the chaotic political situation in Italy at the time. Only the collapse of the wall under the thunderous blows of the demolition ball silences the cacophonous anarchy and brings the musicians back under the control of the director for a brief moment. (Bondanella,1992)

The film ends accordingly:

> with characters locked into master/slave positions. Moreover, the orchestra ends up imprisoned within the abstract signifying system of a single piece of music, which it rehearses over and over – lacking any purpose, it seems, other than repetition, and lacking any audience or point of reference beyond the act of repetition itself. (Burke, 2002, p. 34):

In other words, the tragedy of the eternal child is that his *opera* remains unfinished, and the musicians will never start a real performance. Like eternal children they are impaled in a timeless state, unaware of the passing years, out of tune with time. They therefore understand little of what is gained by repetition and consistency; i.e., by the work of moving back and forth, note by note, tune by tune, left and right, in and out, which makes for subtlety in proceeding step by step through the labyrinthine complexity of the horizontal adult world. The musicians like other eternal children are imprisoned by a circular uroboric circuit, a never ending rehearsal, and like little children remain obedient to their masters, by fear and compliance. Only when submitting to discipline and hard work, can the eternal child develop (Fausto, one of the *vitelloni* has to be beaten by his father to be kept on line, and this beating, "is more than beneficial").

ETERNAL CHILD AS ANTI-HERO

According to James Hillman, in mythology the heroes are usually wanderers, and wandering is a symbol of longing, of the restless urge which never finds what it is seeking. The secret goal of wandering is the symbolic lost mother. One part of the libido, which Jung calls the renegade libido, turns away from heroic tasks and incestuously wishes to go back and down to mother. Blocked by the incest taboo, the libido never finds its goal and so wanders and longs eternally. This dynamic explanation is the early and classical Jungian account of the eternal child: the eternally youthful component of each human being, man or woman, old or young, that is eternally wandering, eternally longing, and is ultimately possessed and attached to the archetypal mother (Hillman, 2005, pp. 180-181).

The mythical path of the *real* hero, also known as the monomyth, is constructed according to a number of stages. The first is leaving one place and going to another. This is a call to begin a journey, an adventure, which the hero must accept. The second involves being tested along the way by obstacles, dangers and challenges which the hero must overcome. The third stage is achieving the goal, thus making new self-consciousness possible. The final and fourth goal is return to the ordinary world, with application of this newly acquired knowledge on a new level of consciousness.

As noted by Joseph Campbell, in this kind of story the real hero dares to leave the ordinary world (Rimini) for regions of supernatural searching (Rome). In the course of his journey, he encounters mythical forces of Nature and achieves a decisive victory. The hero returns from his mysterious journey with the power to distribute the treasures he has brought with him to humanity (Campbell, 1963, p. 30). This could very well reflect the life and character of Fellini, and his gifts of filmography. However, the male characters of the Maestro represent the negatives of his films. They are his anti-heroes.

Initiation is so closely linked to the mode of being of human existence that a considerable number of modern man's acts and gestures continue to repeat initiatory scenarios, like the *vitelloni* without any development and growth. Very often the struggle for life, the ordeals and difficulties that stand in the way of a vocation or a career can reiterate the ordeal of initiation; it is after the blows that are dealt him, the moral and even physical suffering and torture he undergoes, that a young man proves himself, knows his possibilities, grows conscious of his powers, and finally becomes himself, spiritually adult and creative. Every human existence is formed by a series of ordeals, repeated experiences of failure and success, death and resurrection. This is why from a religious standpoint existence is established by painful initiation; human existence is itself an initiation (Eliade, 1987, pp. 208-9). Unlike the eternal child and other Fellinian anti-heroes, a real hero ventures forth from the ordinary world into a region of supernatural wonder: fabulous forces are encountered and a decisive victory is won; the hero comes back from this mysterious adventure with the power to bestow boons on his fellow man (Campbell, 1968, p. 30). He is called to adventure in moment of crisis, and this is the awakening of the self. This can appear also in the midlife. Fellini's first dream dated November 20, 1960, ends with a pressing question from Dr. Bernhard: "Mr. Fellini, do we want to work seriously?" This need to awaken or re-awaken appears in the end of Fellini's life as well. "Wake up!" (*Hei sveglia!!!*) shouts a voice in one of Fellini's dreams in July 1990. In this awakening, the familiar horizon of life has been outgrown. The old concepts, ideals, and emotional patterns no longer fit; the time for the passing of a threshold is at hand (Campbell, 1968, p. 51).The first stage of the mythological journey, the call to adventure, signifies that destiny has summoned the hero and transferred his spiritual center of gravity from within the pale of his society to a zone unknown (Campbell, 1968, p. 58). But often, in actual life, as well as for Fellini's protagonists, the call goes unanswered because it is always possible to turn the other ear. Refusal of the summons converts the adventure into its negative. Walled in by boredom, hard work or culture, the individual (or character) loses the power of significant affirmative action and becomes a victim to be saved. His flowering world becomes a wasteland of dry stones and his life feels meaningless. All he can do is create new problems for himself and await the gradual approach of his disintegration (Campbell, 1968, p. 59). This is the case for Fellini's *vitelloni* and other eternal children like Casanova, Augusto, Marcello, Guido, Checco, Pippo, Snaporaz etc. Fellini's characters were not able to move out of their security zone, their membership in a group, or their immature fantasies.

In mythology, the child and the son were treated as synonyms. *Pueri* were described as trapped in a debilitating relation to the mother, tied to her apron strings or metaphorically devoured and kept effectively out of life by an over-possessive "death-mother". The initial instinctive bond between mother and child then develops into an emotional tie between mother and son that determines the son's path in life long after and despite his having physically flown the coop. Everything continues to turn on the approving or disapproving gaze of the mother. Even in rebellion against the strictures of his own mother, a son who strikes a seemingly heroic and independent pose frequently remains in service of the archetypal Mother through his duty to family, profession, civic and cultural life (all part of the material province of the Great Goddess), with the result that he often unwittingly "avoids his destiny" (Yeoman, 1998, p. 17-18). The archetype of the Great Mother, as presented in Fellini's dreams and works, is a key part of a constellation characterized by the Child and his Hermetic manifestations.

Chapter 5

THE GREAT MOTHER

THE MYTHICAL MOTHER

Although mother is a personal psychological emotional and cognitive experience which has cultural determinants, it also has an archetypal symbolic base expressed in images such as the Great Goddess, Mother Church, the Fates and Mother Nature. The experience of Mother is always influenced by this unconscious template, the Mother archetype. It includes the innate capacity to apprehend and experience nurturance and deprivation, as well as the capacity to symbolize this experience. Mother is more than any human mother can incarnate (Salman, 1997, p. 58).

According to Joseph Campbell, the archetype of the Great Mother is the incarnation of the promise of perfection, the soul's assurance that at the conclusion of its exile in a world of organized inadequacies, we will once again recover the bliss that once was known to us in the remotest past. Time sealed her away, yet she is dwelling still, like one who sleeps in timelessness, at the bottom of the timeless sea. This recollection is not only benign, however. The bad mother is also the absent unattainable mother, against whom aggressive fantasies are directed, and from whom a counter-aggression is feared. She is the hampering, forbidding, punishing mother, the mother who clings to a child who attempts to escape her grasp, the desired but forbidden mother, whose presence is a lure to dangerous desire.

The Mother is at the root of such unattainable great goddess figures (Campbell, 1968, p. 111).The Great Mother is the term for a general image drawn from collective cultural experiences. According to Erich Neumann (1991) the archetype of the Great Mother refers not only to a concrete image existing in space and time, but also to an inner image at work in the human psyche. The impact of this archetype emerges throughout history in the rites, myths and symbols from early civilizations onwards and also in dreams, fantasies and creative work in their relation to the cultural image of the woman. Jung stated that woman, symbolized by the Great Mother, is an unknown planet, the part to which man wants to join, to find a complement, integrity and totality. For the same reason it is the part he knows nothing about. As an image she is characterized by an archetypal fullness but also by a negative polarity.

The configured form of the Great Mother emerges from the primordial archetype and the positive presence of one's own mother. To nourish and protect, to keep warm and hold are the functions in which the elementary nature of motherhood also operates in relation to the child (Neumann, 1991, p. 32). These functions can be symbolically associated with a rock, a cave, a tree, and helpful animals. Hollow objects such as ovens and cooking vessels are associated with the maternal archetype (Jung, 2001, p. 14-15). Fishes, whales and ships that are present in Fellini's filmography and dreams are also attributes of the Great Mother.

The negative pole suggests the bad, devouring Terrible Mother and includes anything secret, hidden and dark such as the abyss, the world of the dead, anything that devours, seduces and poisons, whatever is terrifying and inescapable, like fate or death. The grave, the sarcophagus, deep water, death and decay can be evil aspects of the mother and represent the power of death (Jung, 2001, p. 15). The Great Mother, the creator, was also the black maw that spat man forth and devoured him anew (Paglia, 1990, pp. 8-9). Following Jung, Erich Neumann pointed out that this archetype of the Great Mother can develop into one (more mature) figure which embeds both antithetic qualities simultaneously, like the Greek goddesses of Fate (Moira) or the Aegean Great Goddess, mistress of life and sovereign of death (Neumann, 1991; Neumann, 1994; see mythological examples in Guirand, 1993, pp. 85-86).

Fellini was aware that the mother and the woman in general "is the representation of the eternal symbol of creation" eliciting curiosity and interest but also fear (in Pettigrew, p. 87, my translation). She elicits curiosity and interest, a very complex attitude which involves waiting for a message and not the message itself (p. 88). For the artist, the mother is a source of inspiration, something deeply nourishing (p. 89). She is a source of wonder, fascination but also of terror.

In a number of different articles and interviews, Fellini identified Rome, the Eternal City, as a completely feminine city, combining qualities of the ideal mother and the mistress (Bondanella, 1992, p. 196). For Fellini "Rome is a city indifferent to money, to material success, and also deeply maternal. Mamma Roma always remains an eternal discovery for me" (Pettigrew, p. 143 my translation). The Eternal City, akin to a great mother, keeps her child in her lap. The maternal side of Rome, as well as its indifference, explains why the city never obliges the child to grow up. Romans are thus never neurotic, but they never become adults. The people who frequent the state-controlled brothels do so, according to Fellini, not merely to achieve sexual release but primarily because they want to remain attached as long as possible to a generous and maternal figure who can alleviate their doubts and responsibilities and, above all else, protect them from the difficulties of life. Their ritualistic visits to the brothels, as in the movie *Rome* represent a return to 'the maternal bosom' that indefinitely delays their growth into mature adults. However before the foundation of the city, Romulus and his brother were nursed and nourished by a wild she-wolf. *La lupa* remains the symbol of the city, with her savage feminine parts (for a discussion see Pinkola Estès, 1992, ch.1).

The sketches in Fellini's dream notebooks contain drawings of several such female figures, and they tend to fit the pattern of the Great Mother in that they depict either the erotic sexual bombshell or the terrible and devouring female, and is mostly found in the Eternal City and in particular in archeological sites and its brothels. *The Book* is like a catalogue of Fellinian women and includes buxom matrons "In the most uninhibited poses, taken as a whole the women constitute a joyous element in the director's imagery world: they appear at magic moments, circle round him, arouse him… [with] anxieties, passions and desires" (Kezich, 2008, p. 12).

In Fellini's work there is a profound awareness of the fascinating aspects of Mother Nature. It is impossible to look at his female characters without being puzzled by the grotesqueness of an imagery that nevertheless was totally accepted within the most sublime expression of religion; namely, the Gothic cathedral that elicits fascination, wonder and trembling fear (see discussion in Lopez-Pedraza, 2003, p. 188). In fact the Gothic cathedral of Cologne was supposed to be the static and permanent background of Fellini's movie *Il viaggio di Mastorna* that was never made.

Negative-Positive Polarity of the Great Mother in Fellini's Dream-Work

Fellini's dream-work is replete with archetypal symbolism that can be related to the Great Mother. This is true first of all in terms of her natural counterpart, *Puer* (the Child), and also her derivates, the Hearth and the Kitchen (*Roma, Amarcord)*, Fire (*Satyricon, Amarcord, E la nave va*), the Ship (*Amarcord, E la nave va*), the Moon (*La Voce della Luna*), the Spring and the Fountain (*8½*, *La Dolce Vita*). The embodiment of the Great Mother can also be in a physical woman, who can be everyone and everywhere, who has no name (and sometimes no face), but sometimes nicknames (Gradisca, Anitona, Volpina, Tabaccaia, Saraghina). The use of nicknames implies that these women can be in every village, in every country and at any time. This is valid as well for male protagonists such as the fool of Rimini, Guidizio, whose name in Italian suggests judgment but also wisdom, and whose foolish and grotesque behavior is featured in *Amarcord* and *Clowns*.

These characters are not real people but can be everybody in the collective world or parts of ourselves: Volpina is literally a she-fox, with bestial sexual drives, and Gradisca (literally "please, do") is a woman with strong sex appeal who offers her body and makes a man *pleased*.

Women played an enormous role in Fellini's life, as the eternal object of desire and also as the eternal feminine (Kezich, 2008, p. 11). Suggestive female images are central to Fellini's private fantasy world and dreams (Bondanella, 1992, p. 294). The male presence, which in early films was characterized in the neorealist genre by *Pueri*, the little, immature, unlucky and unemployed cunning dreamers and cheaters (*I vitelloni, Il bidone*, *La dolce vita*), collapses over the years because it is suffocated, broken and crazed by the expansion of feminine bombshells (*La città delle donne*, *La voce della Luna*). In this archetypal equation, the bigger and more inflated the Mother, the smaller, weaker and more eternal the *Puer*. In his filmography, the characters start from tragic, single, pale, a-sexual anti-heroines such as Gelsomina ("with her artichoke-like face") in *La strada* (1954) or the non-erotic and miserable prostitute Cabiria in *Le notti di Cabiria* (1956), or the immature, gullible and infantile wife in *White sheik* during the 1960s. There are also many sick, dead, pale and fragile Giulietta Masinas, the little fairy (*fatina*) in Fellini's dreams during these years. But gradually a variegated parade of erotic female bodies becomes one of the most memorable features of his authorial signature (O'Healy, 2002, p. 209) and dreams. In this process there was a shift from the blond Nordic Valkyrie incarnated in Anita Ekberg into more Oriental, exotic and Mediterranean Great Mothers. *La città delle donne* (City of Women, 1980) can be seen as the most extensive display of these women, in fact in their hundreds. In this movie: "the director seems brought to his knees… by a superior vital force" (Kezich, 2006, p. 345). *City of Women* bears some similarity to the *Casanova's* obsession with women. In both cases the protagonist remains frustrated by his sexuality. In *City of Women* he never performs sexually, while on the other hand, Casanova, as a pathetic Latin lover despite his impressive performances, remain eternally alienated from himself, sad, alone, marginalized and incapable of maintaining an intimate and durable relationship with any women, except for a mechanical doll. This character which differs from the historical Casanova is reminiscent of the personal tragedy of the mythical Pygmalion: "the doll is perfect, she has a living rosy face… I have been looking for you, I want to see what you look like in a natural state" (my translation of a sequence from *Casanova*).

Casanova transforms his sexuality into a pathetic act of competition and performance, as in the scene at Lord Talou's court. Casanova, despite his claim he is "a great poet", becomes a human stud, who can sexually perform at least five times in one hour. But this quantified performance is grotesque, not heroic. His erection remains on the anatomical level not in terms of his psyche and capacity to love as an "erected" mature personality.

GROUPS OF GREAT MOTHERS

In mythology, there are many sub-forms of the Great Mother when women appear in groups. There are women who resemble the primordial elements of Mother Nature who have no cultural or religious meaning. This is the case for the black African dancers who appear in most of Fellini's filmography. They are wild, free and uncontaminated by Christian-colonial-Western culture. In his Satyricon many have something primal, primitive and virginal about them despite their exotic eroticism. They speak an unknown language that can be any language. With their peculiar glossolalia, they are preverbal figures from the unconscious.

In other scenes there are women who are dominated by men; for example the theme of the harem where groups of women are controlled and abused by one man appears in Fellini's filmography (8½, Satyricon and Amarcord). In one of the most significant scenes, Guido (Marcello Mastroianni) cracks a snake whip to get all the women in his real and fantasy life to do his bidding and serve his needs. Sometimes, women in their thousands appear in pictures, like animal trophies of a sexist Don Giovanni (Dr. Kazzone- or Katzone in *La città delle donne*). The name Kazzone is suggestive of a vulgar term in Italian slang for big penis (cazzone). He, as the quintessence of chauvinist phallocentrism, is later arrested and executed by a group of violent feminists. Ettore Manni, the actor who interpreted Katzone, will die after accidentally shooting himself by a gun, during the shooting of the movie… *City of Women*, was released posthumously.

Other types of harems are more classical, such as the Garden of Delights in Fellini's *Satyricon* that is suggestive of the Arabian Nights. The same can be said about the exotic harem in *Amarcord.* Although these harems resemble a masculine fantasy to dominate and be pampered by a group of young women, by contrast other harems can become threatening. Casanova, in Dresden, is raped by a humpbacked voracious woman assisted by three others. One of Fellini's dreams contains a sequence with a castrating harem. This dream may have some "compensation function" in Fellini's psyche, who may have related to women like the dominant Guido, in the *8½* harem scene (Alpert, 1988, p. 167). This dream was reported in 1961, two years before the movie was made:

> I'm a prisoner in a Chinese castle inhabited by extremely expert Chinese prostitutes dressed like geishas. These courtesans are ferociously sadistic, and they know the most refined arts of imaginative and cruel love games, I can hear them all around me, like powerful and treacherous as wild beasts, I can smell the hot breath of their hungry wolves' mouths, they bite my shoulders and arm, with sharp shiny smiles and flashing turbid eyes. …maybe they were playing, they only wanted to arouse me so that they could make love to me. But then I have doubts again: what if they really wanted to kill me? (Fellini, 2008, p. 484)

In other myths, the male protagonist is tossed back and forth by long lines of furies. Like the mythical Bacchantes, Furies, Erinyes and Harpies they represent that aspect of femaleness that clutches, dismembers and kills in order to feed itself a treacherous as wild beast. In *La città delle donne* (1980), an aggressive feminist convention mimics these "thousands of faces, mouths, looks, and voices" (Bondanella, 1992, p. 324). The protagonist seems to float between voracious furies that intend to rape, castrate or execute him. A more protective nymph like Donatella, transmuted into a huge balloon, cannot rescue the male protagonist from his demise. In mythology, the Furies, also called the Erinyes, personified the vengeful moods of the Goddess, a punisher of sinners. Although classical tradition understood the Furies as a symbol of the impersonal functioning of justice, they came to represent men's hidden fear of women, and image apparently still viable (Walker, 1983, p. 327).

Pairs of Great Mothers

Sometimes women appear in pairs, representing antithetic powers, black and white, life and death, as in *Toby Dammit*, where the white young woman incarnates the Devil, and the dark adult one the protector and patroness. In Fellini's *Casanova* the two daughters of Doctor Moebius represent positive and negative aspects of the Great Woman. One is dressed in black, and the other in white. Their bodies are cloaked, like monks, but their faces express lust and sexuality. As assistants to their father, a famous entomologist, they are dedicated to scientific research, and are involved in dissecting and fixing living worms on nails. This vision makes Casanova faint, because he "felt the pain of those demoniac insects". When he loses consciousness he is also treated by these women: "you made me become ill and you gave me back the joy of health". This led to "the sweet death of love" where he declares his intention to run away with Isabella, one of Moebius' daughters.

Again in *Casanova*, his attempted suicide in London was triggered by an altercation with a mother and her daughter, both his lovers. He is not humiliated by their vulgar insults like "exploiter… you and your lies on the stars on horoscopes", but by allusions to his impotence, the negative side of his mental priapism. He loses his will to live when he feels that these women "contaminated what was dearer to me, my health. Filthy syphilis carriers, thieves, leaches… damned Harpies, mortified me, robbed me, destroyed me". Thus pairs of women, women in couples and also single women can draw away sexual power and the will to live.

Great Mothers and Gigantic Bodies

Male characters such as Snaporaz in *Otto e mezzo*, Encolpio in *Fellini's Satyricon*, young Fellini in *Roma*, Fellini's pathetic and narcissist *Casanova*, and the older Snaporaz again in *City of Women* are all eternal children who are portrayed as immature, indecisive and weak male protagonists. The large threatening figures in Fellini's sketches suggest a certain kinship between the

Maestro and his protagonists, especially the more autobiographical ones, at least during his youth (Stubbs, 2006, p. 59). This story line generally involves an inexperienced child or adolescent who is fascinated by a more experienced and bigger/larger/taller female (Bondanella, 1992, p. 294; Stubbs, 2006, pp. 46-47). This type of plot is captured clearly in *Amarcord*, in the libidinal auto-biographical memories of the young Titta, Fellini's alter-ego (Bonnigal, 2002).

Psychologically speaking, spatial deformations such as monstrous gigantism derive from the unconscious blueprint inherited from a time when the observer, the personal and archetypal Child, was indeed tiny relative to others, especially in his relations to his parents, "who must have seemed to scrape the sky" (Gilmore, 2003, p. 175). In psychoanalytical terms, a huge mother creates a sense of terror, impotence and powerlessness. On the other hand, this image is also astounding and enchanting. One of the primordial images used by Fellini in *Clowns* is related to a circus character, a hefty giantess who cannot be defeated by any man. The only person who dares to challenge her force is another woman, allegedly sitting among the public who, under her normal *medio-borghese* dress and female appearance, and despite and her husband's opposition, descends into the circus ring and reveals her Tarzan-like appearance. We never find out who wins but the symbolic meaning is clear: only similar Amazon-like women are able to cope, and outside of this virtual circus may be the only ones to have this unbreakable strength under their weak feminine mask.

This attitude towards the large female body also derives from a typical cultural pattern that shapes Italian masculinity. Probably even the most enlightened Italian man tends to think of women as "the awesome and all-powerful mother", who controls Italian society through her domination of the family (Bondanella, 1992, p. 293). The figure of the gigantic landlady, a typical Italian *matrona*, as she appears in the opening scenes of *Roma*, is a good example of this figure. She rules over her family although (or because?) she is confined to bed "with an inflammation of the ovaries". Her effeminate son, a typical *Puer Aeternus*, an Italian *mammone*, curls up against this enormous mass of feminine flesh in the fetal position: "Fellini suggests with this freakish mother and son that such gigantic Earth Mothers who spend their lives spoiling their male children only succeed in hindering their healthy development into mature heterosexuals" (Bondanella, 1992, p. 196).

This pattern of clinging onto the mother, and curling up in her bosom, persists at least anecdotally among male Italian adults today. Remaining at home with Mamma is reported to be an economic necessity. In an interview in Time Magazine (Burke, 1997), Dr. Laura Sabbadini, a senior researcher at

ISTAT Italian Institute of Statistics, traced the causes of "mammismo" to the fact that more Italians stay longer in school (universities), and that when they get out, they often experience prolonged periods of unemployment. There is also a third dimension, which is the changing nature of the less authoritarian Italian family. This social phenomenon was found to be present in Italy, ten years later (Psychology Today, March, 1st 2008). According to Italian researchers in sociology, eight out of ten Italians aged 18-30 still live at home (cited in MacLeod, 2006):

> In sum, we think that Italian parents put quite a lot of effort into being loved by their children. And to some extent, they buy this love in exchange for their children's giving away some of their independence. Although this might at first sight appear like a mere curiosity, we argue that it has profound economic and social implications.

However these gigantic figures that attract and also capture the Italian male may have universal traits that extend beyond time and space or socio-economical reality. They are not solely an Italian phenomenon, they are universal archetypes. The positive characteristics of the gigantic Great Mother are captured in the vision of a "powerful feminine bust, with wing-shaped arms, joined as though in an act of prayer or in an intimate embrace..." (December, 22, 1961). In one of Fellini's dreams there are certain similarities to a celestial, benevolent Goddess. In particular in the first scene, there is an expression of wonder at the numinous:

> December 1974: Suddenly a marvelous creature wearing a bathing suit appeared, higher than Mount Blanc. She was a woman, a goddess, she looked like (sic). She gazed into the blue sky without seeing us, and from her incredibly beautiful, soft mouth she released an "oh" of wonder and the whole sky filled up white clouds. (Fellini 2008, p. 524)

In the second vision, a similar gigantic image of a benign Goddess displays her attributes of life, fecundity and fertility:

> April 1, 1975 Hypnagogic vision: P. naked and pink like a gigantic newborn, seated on a cloud, immobile in the middle of a bright blue sky. I could feel it was time to intervene and I started blowing on the cloud, saying 'It is time to fertilize what's underneath'. Driven by a powerful breath like that of god, P.'s cloud started floating slowly and calmly through space. P. gathered up her big fabulous breasts in her hands with a solemn gesture, and an ordered, shining rainfall fell on the earth. (p. 527)

In the first two images there is no physical contact between the female subject and the male protagonist of the dream. This is a type of untouchable Olympian divinity who can fertilize the earth. She is inaccessible to normal mortals. In other dreams the Gigantic Woman is more tangible, and is located on Earth, as part of it. She becomes a more available object of desire and sexual attraction. P., a real female figure, appears again in a dream with her sex appeal and grotesque carnality:

> P. has become an enormous, extremely soft form of transportation; lying down, stretched out upon her vast belly, clinging joyously to her immense tits that rise up like round hills in front of me, the great soft body that is wider that the road it is stretched out on, completely nude slips along sweetly like a white vessel, her hips touch the sides of the houses. 'Oh what joy! What a party' I shout 'My great big marvelous whore's hips have gotten even wider! It is wonderful! I love being up here!' (Fellini, 2008, p. 493)

A similar pattern to these dreams can be found in *Fellini's Satyricon*, where intercourse with a Gigantic Mother, Enothea (Enotea), a huge magician (*maga*) with powerful fire between her legs, can deliver fire to human kind and also heal and rehabilitate male impotence. Enothea was bewitched as a punishment for humiliating a more powerful male sorcerer. Her impudence causes the disappearance of fire among humanity, now concealed between her legs. On the one hand, she has lost her strong destructive power, but she now has the power to help humanity by providing light and a hearth. She however lost other faculties when she had to lie in bed and deliver her fire to a line of people. Encolpio confesses his sin to the magician: "I have killed a man, I have desecrated a temple, and now I am a soldier without his weapon". By copulating with her, Encolpio can again declare that he "has the scepter which functions again". Thus thanks to Enothea, a service is rendered by a "Generous Mother" with the help of Priapus/Hermes, the same god who punished Encolpio for his sin of killing the hermaphrodite.

In some of Fellini's dreams, the Gigantic Mother, a big, fat, blubbery figure, elicits different feelings including ambivalence, in particular regret, repulsion and disgust mixed with pleasure and appeasement. The Goddess becomes a more earthly and abject whore-like figure. The first dream shows both disgust and attraction related to the sexual act:

> ...a great big glorious old whore... I regret having called the big hooker; up closer she is older, with broken teeth. I'm disgusted by the

> idea of sticking my penis in her mouth... I realize that the big whore's flesh is white, tender, very pleasurable. It is impossible to resist her; her blubber bestows peace and sleep. (Fellini, 2008, p. 472)

In the second dream, animal features (a wolf pelt and a little monkey) are related to the female image. This sexual encounter is frustrated or interrupted and leaves marks on the body of the male protagonist, Fellini, the dreamer:

> Sandrocchia wearing the white wolf outfit like the character of Susy wore, rounder, fatter. She puts her soft belly against mine and I touch her big fabulous elastic thighs with great pleasure. We look for a quiet place where we can make love. We can't find one, what anger! In any case, first I have to get rid of a small black and white monkey that moves my left hand. .. it left a mark of its sharp little teeth. (Fellini, 2008, p. 498)

Themes of ambivalence toward the Gigantic Body can be found in several of Fellini's movies. Perhaps the most famous imagery in all of Fellini's filmography appears in *La dolce vita*, when Marcello (Mastroianni) exclaims to Sylvia, the Nordic Blond Beauty (Anita Ekberg), while hugging her in the (baptismal) waters of *Fontana di Trevi*, that she is "everything. The first woman on the first day of creation, you are the sister, the lover, the friend, the *angel* and the *devil*... you are: the Hearth" (my translation and italics).

The waters symbolize spring and origin, the reservoir of all the possibilities of existence; they precede every form and support every creation. On the other hand, immersion in water signifies regression to the pre-formal, reincorporation into the undifferentiated mode of pre-existence. Emersion repeats the cosmogonic act of formal manifestation; immersion is equivalent to a dissolution of forms. This is why the symbolism of the waters, as in *Fontana di Trevi*, signifies both death and rebirth (Eliade, 1987, p. 130).

In Fellini's *Intervista*, during the meeting between Marcello and Anita 27 years later, Sylvia's gigantic mythical image is preserved. She is big, huge, covered only by a blanket. She is "wonderful like a gladiator". The camera films her from ground level, giving a child-like view of her gigantic dimensions. For old Marcello, Anita still remains: "Eve, the first woman who appeared on the earth."

A similar ambivalence combining heaven/earth, angel/devil, human/ beast (or woman covered with fur), life/death, protection/abandonment, prayer/intimate embrace, Madonna/whore, can be found in other dreams related to the actress Anita Ekberg. These dreams appeared at different times in Fellini's life. The first reported by the author dates to November 1966:

> I am making love to N. and Anita. N. is on top of me but my member is in Anita's big pussy, and I finally see her enjoy it. Ah! What a pleasure, her clear little girl's eyes spoiled and cruel, fog over with the orgasm, her lids come down as if to veil her ecstatic enjoyment...Finally! But then the big Valkyrie, though continuing to ride me, turns her back to me. 'What a whore' I think 'She's already gotten dressed so that she doesn't waste any time'. She is wearing a fur on her head, in a minute she's going to dump me so that she can run off to another client. (Fellini, 2008, p. 504)

Fellini's memories in *8½* also capture the ambivalence of a child's attraction to the natural and wild sides of the giantess/prostitute (La Saraghina). He spies on her secretly and dances with her on the beach near the parochial school he attended. He is enchanted but also punished by his bigoted teachers for having seen the incarnation of the Devil. The image of the Saraghina can be related to Fellini's first personal revelation of the erotic woman, and his capacity to explore the unconscious (a wild area outside the civilization of the town). When aged ten, he really encountered:

> ...a plump, unkempt woman who, they knew, traded her favors for sardines brought back by the local fisherman. The boys pooled the funds for the opportunity to lift her skirts... to reveal a fullness of flesh. Saraghina (the 'sardine girl'), is the name Fellini gave her, as she persisted in his memory as his first image of sexuality. (Alpert, 1988, pp. 20-21)

The Gigantic Woman sometimes has a big mouth and tongue and can devour everybody. This image is captured in a *schizzo* of a dream (Fellini 2008, p. 553). The author writes "I don't remember the plot of the dream". But the picture is very impressive: the image of a gigantic woman's head that is going to swallow a bartender by sticking out her long tongue. As stressed by Gilmore (2003, p. 176), the colossal mouth, as an organ of predation and destruction, is closely related to physical immensity.

The same positive-negative polarity of an angel-devil female figure deriving from her vagina and womb can be seen in the opening sequence of *Casanova* (1976). Here Fellini deals with the Mediterranean Mother "the mysterious female who lives in each of us" (cited in Bondanella, 1992, p. 309). The large statue of Venus/Venice which appears in the first sequence of the movie that shows the carnival of Venice has the attracting-terrifying potential for procreation all women possess that makes men insecure in their presence, because the female reveals to man his own incapacity to give birth to new life, with the mysteries of her womb. The first scene depicts a ritual that unfolds at night on the Grand Canal, from whose depths emerges the gigantic black head of a woman. Venus/Venice is a kind of deity of the lagoon. In a hymn to this huge archetypal figure the male public praises the "Mona (cunt), screwer and defecating ass, subterranean old hag" but also the "great cunt, powerful cunt, coquette and embroiler who is given to us by lot as bride and mother, wicked mother in law and stepmother, sister and grandmother, daughter and Madonna" (translated in Bondanella, 1992, p. 310). This is a hymn either to a pure queen (*oh regina!*) or a beautiful whore (*bela putona!*): "old smelly woman, Big Mona flirter and cheater". This is a Madonna/Whore image. Her disappearance back into the Laguna is a disaster because "we will never see her again" (my translation). She can emerge and sink back into the abyss.

Four years before making *Casanova*, the director described the following dream, which hints at the scene in the movie, and may stress negative aspects of this Goddess of the Sea. According to Ravasi Bellocchio (2009), this is a typical Big Dream embedded by strong archetypal forces. The Goddess in fact can give life but also take life:

> I saw the scene broadcast on television: an enormous stone statue lies half sunken at the sea's edge, corroded by time and seawater. It must be extremely ancient and portrays a woman with her eyes closed. A goddess? A queen? The corpse of a little seven or eight-year-old girl is draped over the statue. She was killed by the sea waves, which tossed her violently against the stone effigy. The mother… cries her desperation, punching the head of the statue with one fragile hand as if in her mad pain she wanted to take revenge by smashing the stone apart (Fellini, 2008, p. 517)

Different versions of the theme of the Great Mother have been used by other directors influenced by Fellini icons. In Woody Allen's *Oedipus Wrecks* (in *New York Stories*, 1989), a caricature of a huge Jewish Mother appears in the sky. She is omnipotent and omniscient, over-protecting, snoops into her son's affairs, and alternatively teases and praises him. She concretizes as a human being only when the neurotic son follows her admonitions and finds a nice Jewish girl. In 2002, forty years after Fellini's *Antonio's temptations*, the Spanish Director Pedro Almodovar, in his *Talk to her*, develops a scene in which the male hero shrinks and takes a walk on his lover's body. In this case the breasts become mountains to climb, and the vagina becomes a gate, where the protagonist disappears.

The mouth and vulva are equated in many myths. Mouth comes from the same root as mother, vulvas have lips. Many men believe that behind the lips lie teeth. To Christian ascetics, hell's mouth and the vagina drew upon the same ancient symbolism. Both were equated with the womb symbol of the fish or the whale that swallowed Jonah. In Jewish tradition a silent woman is a sign of purity and modesty.

The archetypal image of the devouring female seems undeniably alive even in the modern world. Psychoanalysts have argued that males in Western culture are afraid of direct contact with female genitalia, and are even afraid of referring to these genitalia themselves entering the female mouth, or other orifices seems fraught with hidden fears, signified by the confusion of sex with death in overwhelming numbers of male minds and myths. Psychiatrists say sex is perceived as little death the death of the *little man*, the penis (Walker, 1983, pp. 1034-6).

Themes of reciprocal engulfment, to possess and being possessed appear in Fellini's *Casanova*. For example, when he speaks about the meaning of kissing he claims that "the kiss is just the desire to devour what is kissed, [but also] to get lost in the soul of the woman you love".

ORALITY: THE BREAST

As seen in the second dream quoted in this chapter, the symbolism of the nurturing and fertilizing breast is a basic attribute of the Goddess. This image seems to be rooted in the genesis of all living beings. As Yalom points out: "in the beginning was the breast. For all but a fraction of human history, there was no substitute for a mother's milk... prehistoric statuettes were, in all likelihood, fertility goddesses, mother goddesses, or nursing goddesses" (1998, p. 9).

But the breast, even in its direct relation to milk, can also have ambivalent powers, as stressed in certain trends in psychoanalytic theory (Melanie Klein for example) in that it can poison, abandon or waken uncontrollable sexual drives. In the short movie *Le tentazioni del dottor Antonio* (1961), which marked Fellini's first use of color, Fellini shows the deleterious effects of the Great Mother's breast and its milk on a bigoted puritan. He becomes possessed by a billboard poster advertising milk that depicts an enormous and sexually suggestive image of Anita Ekberg's breast. On the one hand, the emphasis on the innocuous commercial jingle, sung by children, "drink more milk, it does you good" (*bevete più latte, il latte fa bene*) implies primal maternal breastfeeding and nurturing. However the vision that Antonio experiences finally destroys his middle-class respectability and religious bigotry by releasing destructive sexual drives through a morbid attraction to the sexual breast of the gigantic woman. In this sense, the symbol of the "good" breast, with the accent on its ability to nurse and nourish not only infants, becomes a "bad" one, as an agent of enticement for male adults (Yalom, 1998, p. 4), and later, of destruction. Antonio repressed these drives until his encounter with the billboard. To use a Freudian term he developed the defense mechanism of "reaction formation" to his sexual drives, a reaction which drove him to his Catholic puritan crusade against the billboard. The resulting conflict between his strict morality and his unconscious desires ends in madness. The gigantic Ekberg incarnates into a human being, bigger than the city, and picks up Antonio in her huge hand, thus bringing him close to her chest like King Kong in reverse. There is a striking contrast between Anita's enormous breast size and the puny figure of Antonio beginning to strip naked. In the final scenes, Antonio, completely insane, possessed in psychoanalytical terms by all of his repressed sexuality, dresses up in the armor of Saint George fighting the dragon. In his losing battle, he throws his phallic lance at Anita's breast, and goes mad (Bondanella, 1992, p.159-163). In the last scene, in a symbiotic state "don't take her from me, she is mine" in a naked fetal position (like a *Pietà* painting) pinned down on the billboard, he is rescued by an ambulance and hospitalized.

A similar dynamics of possession by forces of the female breast is present in the movie *Amarcord* (1974), when the young adolescent Titta hugs the huge breast of the Tobacconist (*la Tabaccaia*) his object of fantasies and desire. However, instead of "sucking" (*succhia stupido!*), as the large woman tells him to do, he just blows out into the breast. This experience leaves him "deflated", emptied, weakened, mortified by the woman, and the day after he falls sick.

Anality: The Buttocks

The female buttocks and anus are a central theme in Fellini's dream-work. Their functions and penetrability are a fixed idea in his filmography and probably in his erotic fantasies. These body parts can be seen as a fundament, like the bottom, that hold ups, supports and provides the foundation for the higher areas in the image of the Great Mother (see for example: Miller 1997, p. 100). In Italian slang, having an ass (*avere culo*), means being a lucky person, or in mythological terminology, being blessed by Hermes, the god of windfall and luck.

For *Casanova* the ass is his best friend, and its image (of a young woman) is the only stratagem to perform sexually with an old and ugly noblewoman, the Marchesa d'Ufrà.

The primal memories of attraction to big buttocks appear in *Amarcord*, with scenes of young peasants' buttocks riding bicycles, as well as *La città delle donne*, where the most significant image of the first sexual experience of the protagonist, Snaporaz in his adolescence was his first visit to a bordello. The buttocks of the prostitute are filmed as a close-up that fills the whole screen, while her face is concealed behind big glasses so that she has no presence, even from the start.

Buttocks are not only a primal memory of youth in Fellini's work. They still attract and obsess the aged Marcello Mastroianni playing the character of the old, poor, pathetic and drunk Pippo in *Ginger and Fred* (1985). As a hobby he likes to invent sad, vulgar rhymes on this theme, as for example: *Donna senza culo/e' come alpino senza mulo* (A woman without an ass is like an alpinist [soldier in the First World War] without a mule, my translation). Titta's grandfather in *Amarcord* never misses an opportunity to touch and pinch the house-maid's buttocks (and to fart).

One of Fellini's dreams takes a positive attitude toward the Great Mother's posterior:

> I open my arms to her and Sofia, an expensive domestic prostitute, immediately takes me into the kitchen… Sofia lies down with me on the sofa, around us there's an atmosphere that's so familiarly whorish that I feel happy, how happy I am with this triumphant large-butted woman, among the stovetops of this kitchen and the smells of a good dinner that the pleasant old prostitute is preparing! 'This is truly my woman!' I think and Sofia turns her vast, marvelous butt to me… finally I gloriously take Sofia. (Fellini, 2008, p. 479)

In another dream there is more ambivalence toward a prostitute with beastlike behavior (Fellini, 2008, p. 474): " the big-butted nighttime street walker … you can hear the big beautiful whore's laugh unpleasantly, disturbing, wolfishly."

Forms of anality depicted as orifices in the female body can also lead to tranquility and happiness, a childish pampering, spoiling, and a soothing feeling of being in the Hearth and the Kitchen. However, like wild animals and body parts such as the mouth or the vagina, the rectum, beside its scatological functions, can contain and imprison the male body. In a dream dated 1975 the figure of the last Italian King is restrained inside the orifice of a Great Mother:

> There was a tiny war taking place on the beach, and from my boat I could see small infantrymen with the uniforms of the 1915-1918 war throwing incredibly small bombs. Then Lea arrived, completely naked. She was stupendous, powerful, tanned. She knelt down near the sea, and with her hands separated her giant butt cheeks from one another. Vittorio Emanuele the Third stuck his head out of that giant fabulous butt. And Lea laughing her heart out of the middle of the bright sunlight shouted to me: 'PIPETTO'S HERE WITH HIS FLAG TOO!!! MAYBE NOW THEY'LL STOP WITH ALL THESE WARS!!'" (capitals in the text) (Fellini, 2008, p. 526)

GENITALITY: THE VAGINA AND THE WOMB

For Jung the so-called incest prohibition goes back to something much more fundamental. The incest prohibition prevents a son from symbolically reproducing himself through the mother. Jung claimed however that the basis of "incestuous desire is not cohabitation, but the strange idea of becoming a child again, of returning to the parental shelter, and of entering into the mother in order to be reborn through her... it is not incestuous cohabitation that is desired, but rebirth" (Jung, 1957, p. 223-224). In classic psychoanalytical theory, aside from incest fantasies, re-entering the womb may also be the deepest repressed desire of any man; namely, to return to the origin. As Ferenczi stressed, sexual intimacy, and the desire to merge with the woman's body and penetrate her can be seen as desire to return to the womb (Ferenczi, 1989) and be reborn. This theme is developed by Almodovar's protagonist in *Talk to her*, who, as a shrunken man, gets naked, opens a breach into his lover's vagina and disappears into his lover's womb.

In a sequence towards the end of *Casanova* when the hero decides to commit suicide and walks into the Thames with rocks in his pockets, he spots a gigantic woman, the princess Hiawatha on the shore and decides to live, and follows her to a nearby circus. In this case, his gaze and later peeping at her naked when being bathed by her two dwarf attendants saves his life. More information about this woman makes Casanova even happier. She is the tallest and strongest woman in the world ("seven feet tall"), a Fury who can throw eight strong men to the ground, but in particular Casanova can integrate the dichotomy between her as a strong "creature from mythology" and a delicate human being, abandoned by her husband, a native of the same region as Casanova ("Venetian but from the mountains"), an earthly maternal woman who, when bathing, assisted by two dwarfs, softly sings a lullaby.

In one of the sequences, Casanova does not realize that the woman has disappeared into the body of an enormous (female) whale. Casanova sees a long line of men marching silently into the mouth of the whale, called by a circus barker "La Grande Mona [Cunt]". The whale is clearly a euphemistic image for the female womb. The theme of big fish and whales recurs in Fellini's filmography (see for example the final scene in *La Dolce Vita*). The fish is worldwide symbol of the Great Mother and her womb. Fish and womb were synonymous in Greek: Delphos meant both (Walker, 1983, p. 313). Inside the body of the protective whale womb, Casanova encounters a magic lantern show projecting frightening drawings of the *vagina dentata*. They depict the female sexual organ as a vortex into which men are dragged, like a spider web (Bondanella, 1992, p. 315). The giantess Casanova followed into the whale/womb and whom he meets there inside the animal's belly extends the theme of ambivalence to the womb/vagina of the Great Mother (see discussion in Miller, 1997; Creed, 1993, ch. 4, 8). Braun and Wilkinson (2001) suggest that negative representations of the vagina can include the vision of a passive receptacle for the penis, something sexually inadequate, disgusting, vulnerable and abused but also dangerous. Stories of the devouring mother are ubiquitous in myths, representing the death fear which the male psyche often transforms into a sex fear. In *Casanova* "The Mona is an oven that burns everything". In Venetian dialect the term "*va' in mona!*" can be loosely translated into "go to hell!" However in Italian slang, *essere sfigato* (not having a *figa* or *fica*, a vagina), means being unlucky, unprotected by mother nature. Thus vernacular forms in Italian slang and dialects till conserve this popular ambivalence toward the vagina, luck vs. misery.

Male fear of women is crystallized by the magic lantern Casanova sees in the whale of a vagina with teeth, the vagina that bites off and swallows the (erect and penetrating) penis. The vagina is the hidden orifice that castrates 'post-coitus'. In these pictures female sexuality is constructed as an untamed and wily site of danger and horror not least of all because it is hidden from sight. It is an expression of terror of the Great Mother. Clearly the descent into the *mona* leads Casanova to a frightening confrontation with a part of the mystery of sexuality that Jungians believe exists at least for males. As a pathetic Don Juan, Casanova can still discover shadow-parts of the feminine. Woman can be seen as: "a mediatrix who tries to lead Casanova to a discovery of the unconscious...she has done her office" (Stubbs, 2006, p. 63-64).

Some parallels to these images can be found in Fellini's dreams and are suggestive of his fear of *vagina dentata*. In the first dream the vagina gives birth to a little monster with its own maw:

> November 1967: Giulietta has to give birth to 'a golden shark'. She's already having labor pains … and I see a shark's scythe-like tail emerge from between her legs. I yell at everybody to stand back because the shark is ferocious and voracious even as a newborn... The shark flops around on the ground, I insist on warning everybody to be careful but I'm not really convinced the little monster is really ferocious, in fact taking a better look at it seems to be a rubber toy. (Fellini 2008, p. 513)

In the second dream the vagina devours and engulfs important information (or parts of the male ego?) in a different way:

> It was necessary to find a little page from a notebook where some generalities had been written down- numbers and general information about a friend of mine, a great friend, so important and close that I though perhaps that it … was me. A. swallowed that little page… and was even willing to give it back, but at the same time she claimed never to have seen it and therefore never to have swallowed it. Now she was quiet, her face wearing that inscrutable expression of a goddess chased out of the bosom of Olympus. She was enormous, incredibly beautiful, entirely naked, her colossal thighs spread wide, her big fabulous tits partially gathered into her two hands. I was naked too, red with pleasure and embarrassment, and I got ready to search her vagina for that little page covered with information…will I be able to find it? (Fellini 2008, p. 542)

Ravasi Bellocchio notes that the Italian term for generality (in Italian generalità), means one's personal details or particulars (like on an identity card). This term is suggestive of the core of the person and the place where he was "generated". This can be seen as a Big Dream, which is behind "the unconscious world of the dreamer, to disclose meanings that concern humanity" (2009, pp. 110-111, my translation). In fact the term generality has the same etymologic root as genes, janitors, genealogy, genetics, progeny, genitalia and generation, etc.

In *La voce della luna* (*The Voice of the Moon*, 1990) the same negative-positive polarity relates to the vagina and voracious genital sexuality in the figure of Marisa. Initially she is very attractive and friendly to her spineless husband, Nestore. She can awaken sexual desire and the potent sexual act is similar to the power of a steam engine, like "a locomotive". O'Healy writes that she is one of the most spectacular configurations of a sexually desiring woman. When female genital desire exceeds male need, it is almost always represented as threatening or grotesque (O'Healy, 2002, p. 225). She is a tall woman wearing a tight red suit with a plunging fur (animal) collar, alternately fearful and flirtatious. Later she shows herself to be a calculating personality, a voracious woman (she leaves Nestore for a rich butcher), as she waits in the *piazza* to supervise the emptying of the apartment she once shared with Nestore. She has robbed him of all his possessions; in other words she has annihilated him. In various scenes, Nestore seems to have shrunk in stature and Marisa looms even larger than before (p. 226). She can manipulate him for her needs, and when she leaves him he remains abandoned without any power (impotent, castrated), broken and penniless. She leaves Nestore shattered and "dismembered" (by a *butcher* mistress with a vagina with teeth).

In a dream dated July 14th, 1974, Fellini depicts the negative chthonic, decaying features of the Great Mother, which may have some similarities with the symbolism of the opening scene and the finale in *8½*. It involves a cave instead of a tunnel:

> Where the old flower market used to be international recording (sic), there's an immense cavern filled with smashed public urinals and toilets. A rather sluttish girl brought me there, and I stare at the foul smelling building, shocked and disgusted. The stench is atrocious. With great indignation, I see that at the back of this great putrid grotto there's a long stand with freshly baked bread. There is even an oven back there. I nibble on a piece of bread in that horrendous air wet with urine and discover that the bread itself is soggy, as if it were soaked… I complain, scandalized, resentful, but the girls behind the stand do not answer, they seem shocked that I dare to criticize a situation that everyone else accepts as normal…(Fellini 2008, p. 520)

In this situation, which is collective or universal ("international") rather than personal, there are facets of the womb of Terrible Mother Earth. Despite the potential of maternal nurturing (the oven, the bread), and growth in the protective womb (a place where flowers are sold), women become dissolute and impure and edible products like bread undergo a process of decay, filth and putridity. In these images, the belly or womb of the earth is symbolized not only by subterranean darkness such as hell and night but also by tunnels, caves and grottos (see discussion in Neumann 1991, p. 44).

The cave was universally identified with the womb of Mother Earth, the logical place for symbolic birth and regeneration. Etruscan and Roman temples featured a subterranean *mundus*, meaning both earth and womb. Holy places in Hinduism were caves representing the Great Mother (Walker, 1983, p. 154-5).

However, areas related to the underground, such as sewers, underground streams, caves, graves, etc. can indicate positive qualities of birth: there is an old Latin saying that we are born from urines and feces: *Inter urinas and feces nascimur*. The manure and the dung are the fertilizers of the soil. In Fellini's *Roma* people are seen eating with gusto during a banquet in the streets of Trastevere while exposed to the stink from the underground sewers. In *E la nave va* the passengers are exposed to the rhino's unbearable stench. The rhino is located in the belly of the ship. Again, it can symbolize unconscious material, which should be discovered and brought up on the bridge to be washed and approached by the passengers. In the final scene of the movie we are informed that this animal can even supply tasty milk.

The image of the smelly rhino is reminiscent of the idea that other animals brought to the surface can decay. Both the big fish in the last scene of *La dolce vita*, or the whale in *Satyricon* and *Casanova* are taken from the depth of the sea to the surface, and can elicit a new level of consciousness. But when these animals are taken to the surface they can also decay, dry up and become putrid. The unconscious is nourished by confusion, the unexpected, and an immobility that makes us afraid. This is why we need to explore these dark zones and to carefully descend into these areas, into the depths of the sea. Suppressing the unconscious is like mutilating ourselves, or losing the nourishing potential of animals when they are kept in their natural place. The sun, i.e. the symbol of rationality, destroys these forces, as well the healing powers of the hermaphrodite in *Satyricon*.

In *Roma*, the excavation for the subway leads to the discovery of catacombs (with 400 skeletons) and also the appearance of *villa romana* frescos, with vivid portraits of the householders which even after 2000 years are still vivid. For a few minutes the reporters and the technical team in charge of the excavation have a numinous primal contact with ancient knowledge preserved pristinely in the womb of the earth, close to a subterranean river (Bondanella, 1992, p. 197). A phallus-shaped mechanical device called a "mole", which resembles a dildo or a vibrator far more than a real construction drill, reveals an ancient Roman home to Fellini's crew. But it is a woman journalist who warns the crew that this penetration into the depth of the earth will destroy the fresco. In fact, the gusts of air churned by the phallic mole will make many frescos fade. Thus once again we learn from Fellini that the journey into the unconscious is a dangerous affair, and most of the material will be lost on the way.

Chapter 6

FELLINI'S LIFE AND WORKS

Federico Fellini (January 20, 1920 - October 31, 1993) was an Italian film director, the author of screen plays, books and a caricaturist. He is considered one of the most influential and highly revered filmmakers of the 20th century, and influenced the works of Ingmar Bergman, Akira Kurosawa, Woody Allen and Pedro Almodovar.

Fellini was born on January 20, 1920 to middle-class parents in Rimini, then a small town in the Romagna region on the Adriatic Sea, a well known tourist destination for Northern Europeans. His father Urbano was a traveling salesman and wholesale vendor, who, permissive but absent, was not involved in the education of his children. His mother, Ida, was more unflappable and severe, begging her children to behave (Kezich, 2006, p. 12).

In 1924, under the Fascist regime of Benito Mussolini, Fellini started Catholic primary school in Rimini, but was sent to public school two years later. He was an average pupil, marginally attracted by the cinema. As a child he often experienced dream-like states, a sense of physical vibration in particular when in bed. This capacity to withdraw from reality and go deep into a hypnagogic state would characterize him for his entire life. Sometimes these experiences were successful, leaving Fellini with a sense of wonder and happiness. But sometimes he felt dragged down by a sense of heaviness, as though he were rooted to the ground.

In the majority of archaic religions, flights or what Fellini called his "usual vibrations" signifies access to a superhuman mode of being (god, magician, ghost, spirit). It basically suggests freedom to go wherever one wants and is thus an appropriation of the condition of the spirit (Eliade, 1987,

p. 176). This Fellinian quality is reminiscent of the attributes of the Greek god Hermes, a theme which characterizes most of this book.

It is interesting to indicate that Jung stressed, in his childhood experienced, a number of visual hallucination, he also appeared to have had the capacity to evoke images voluntarily. Jung's *Red Book* (2009), can be seen, similarly to Fellini's *Book of Dreams*, as a personal confrontation with the unconscious to get to the bottom of his inner process, to translate the emotions into images to grasp the fantasies which were stirring underground. Of course the style of the *Red Book* is different, because of its ornamental borders, illustrated initials, medieval illuminated manuscripts with calligraphic writing. It also includes many mandalas and geometric shapes.

In 1926, Federico Fellini discovered the world of the circus. In 1927 hagiography suggests he ran away with a circus clown called Pierino although his relatives later denied this story. If in fact Fellini did flee, it was purely psychological: he had been hooked by the magic world of the circus for his entire life. For Fellini, clowns did not only parody a specific order of society but represented a more universal human need to overturn reality (Free, 1973, p. 215).

Enrolled in a high school for classical studies (*liceo classico*) in 1929, he became a member of the compulsory Fascist youth movement, but he was never a militant or a involved in Fascism. It was at school that he developed a taste for humor and caricature, mocking institutions, in particular the state, the church, the family and the school. He was the leader of a gang of fourteen juvenile troublemakers. They booed and made sarcastic remarks at workers. In the early hours of the morning they woke up monks at a monastery by shooting water pistols at their cells and they teased young lovers who had sought privacy behind boats on the beach (Alpert, 1988, p. 24). Although he failed his military culture exam, Fellini graduated from high school (*maturità classica*) in July 1938 after taking the exam over. In 1938 Fellini's first drawing and several short articles were published in the prestigious newspaper *Domenica del Corriere* and the Florentine weekly *420*.

Fellini's departure from Rimini on March 1939 was his first confident step into the vast world. His actual exit was not nearly as poetic, at least according to the friends he left behind. They insulted him affectionately in the local *Romagnolo* slang, calling him *pataca* - a jerk - saying that he was not even leaving alone but with a group. Fellini considered his arrival in Rome as a liberation from the oppressive *provincia* and portrayed this in famous scenes in a number of his movies (*Roma, The White Sheik, Ginger and Fred*). In *Roma* a dark slender young man gets off a train and wanders through the chaos of the city with bulging Alice-in-Wonderland eyes (Kezich, 2006, p. 21-2). Fellini went to Rome to start a career in journalism and also, as he was to say later, in search of himself (Alpert, 1988, p. 32). It was a dramatic step in a quest for an identity separated from his family, his peers and his past. He thus began his mythical *hero* journey, his personal path which was to include many ordeals. Living in the Eternal City was unlike any other. As C.G. Jung wrote in his *Memories, Dreams, Reflections*:

> I always wonder about people who go to Rome, as they might go, for example, to Paris or to London. Certainly Rome as well as these other cities can be enjoyed aesthetically; but if you are affected to the depth of your being at every step by the spirit that broods there, if a remnant of a wall here and a column there gaze upon you with a face instantly recognized, then it becomes another matter entirely.(1963, pp. 268-9)

In September 1939, Fellini enrolled at the University of Rome law school to comply with his parents' middle-class expectations, although he never attended a class. Installed in a family-style hotel a "*pensione*", he started to draw sketches of restaurant and café patrons. Four months afterwards he published his first article in *Marc'Aurelio*, the highly influential biweekly humor magazine. Later he joined the editorial board, and wrote a regular column entitled *Will You Listen to What I Have to Say?* He was employed steadily from 1939 to 1942, interacting with writers, gagmen, and scriptwriters. These contacts eventually led to opportunities in show business and cinema. In 1940, the year Italy entered World War II on the side of the Axis powers against France and England, he began writing radio sketches and gags for films, but still wrote screenplays and articles for satirical magazines.

While writing for radio as a way to evade the draft, Fellini met his future wife Giulietta Masina in the studio office of the Italian Radio Broadcasting Corporation, in the autumn of 1942. His wife described him as a lanky, skinny young man with long hair and sparkly eyes, who was charming and funny. Fellini's bohemian friends were initially surprised that he had fallen for a woman so physically different from the flashy, voluptuous girls he had always been attracted to, and who later were known as the "Fellini type" or the Fellinian-Fellinesque character. However Fellini felt Giulietta had an elfin aura that made him happy (Kezich, 2006, p. 50). Many years later, in one of his dreams she still appears as infantile, delicate and pretty as she was when they met, like a little fairy (October 8, 1961). After dating for nine months, the couple got married on October 30, 1943. Several months later, Masina suffered a miscarriage. She gave birth to a son but the child died of encephalitis three weeks later. This tragedy had enduring emotional and artistic repercussions and remained a painful chapter in the couple's life. They would never have children. Years later Fellini would still refuse to discuss it. Among the couple most intimate friends, many speculated that the tragedy strengthened their spiritual union but prematurely ended their physical relationship (Kezich, 2006, p. 74).

After the Allied liberation of Rome on June 4, 1944, Fellini and a friend opened the *Funny Face Shop* where they survived the postwar recession drawing caricatures of American soldiers for money. He continued working as a screenwriter, and also took on occasional jobs as assistant director, working as both screenwriter and assistant director for the famous Italian director Roberto Rossellini. In February 1948, he was introduced to Marcello Mastroianni, then a young theater actor appearing in a play with Giulietta Masina.

When Fellini first came to the world of cinema he irritated people by openly rejecting all beliefs, political affiliations and ideologies. He was in fact almost apolitical – at least in terms of how the notion of being political was presented, or rather imposed, during the Fascist era. He was equally distant later from as the ruling Christian Democracy party, its leftist socialist-communist opposition and intellectual militant activism in general. Politics and soccer left Fellini feeling bored like a "little boy listening to adult conversation" (Kezich, 2006, p. xiv). One of his dreams captures his desire to rip away the hypocritical façade of politicians or political leaders:

> Garibaldi [the Italian hero of independence] is dying. He's in bed with the same face he always has in history books and on postage stamps… It always seems like a plastic mask "I want to die with my real face!" shouts Garibaldi suddenly. "Enough of this mask already! Enough of this foolishness! At least when I'm dying I want my real face". And tearing himself away from those who want to prevent him, Garibaldi rips his age-old mask off his face, and underneath a younger, friendly, more virile face appears. Having watched the entire scene, I applaud enthusiastically, moved and sympathetic. And I tell Liliana that Garibaldi did the right thing, that's what he should have done, finally, good job, Garibaldi, good job! (Dream, October 18, 1974)

Fellini received numerous prizes and awards, including a final Oscar *ad honorem* for his life's work. However the Maestro often had to deal with the criticism of leftist activists who rejected his tolerant attitude to neo-realism, as well as the concerns of the Church and the Vatican over his vulgar eroticism and implicit anti-clericalism. He also elicited the ire of militant feminists for his representation of women as an object of male sexuality (in particular in his

City of Women). However even as a young caricaturist and cartoonist, Fellini expressed himself through his sarcastic humor, and was more in tune with his inner voice than the latest trends, fashion or ideologies *di regime*.

His loyalty to his inner world and his capacity to direct his actors to be attuned to it, made Fellini the director who came the closest to an inner and universal truth that transcends political beliefs, cultural biases or assumptions and gendered relations. Fellini believed in spontaneous chance meetings, love affairs, and friendships – all of which he encountered with astounding ease. They were constant revelations which he deliberately nurtured. He lived inside of things with indomitable curiosity and unflappable openness. He abandoned himself to what Dostoevsky called the "river of life". He was serenely aware that the river always carried you somewhere, despite the sense of confusion (Kezich, 2006, p. xv).

In 1950 Fellini co-produced and co-directed his first feature film *Variety Lights* (*Luci del varietà*) with Alberto Lattuada, which reflected his interest in the world of vaudeville. Its release was met with poor reviews, and a limited distribution proved disastrous for all concerned. The production company went bankrupt, leaving both Fellini and Lattuada with debts to pay for over a decade. Fellini began production of *The White Sheik* in September 1951, his first solo-directed feature. Starring the young actor Alberto Sordi in the title role, the film is based on the life of *fotoromanzi*, the photographed cartoon strip romances popular in Italy at the time. In 1953, *I vitelloni,* episodes in the life of wayward, mature male loafers in provincial Rimini found favor with the critics and the public. It won the Silver Lion Award in Venice, and secured Fellini's first international distributor.

Fellini directed *La strada* based on a script completed in 1952. During the last three weeks of shooting, Fellini experienced the first symptoms of severe clinical depression. Aided by his wife, he undertook a brief therapy with Freudian psychoanalyst Emilio Servadio.

In 1955, Fellini cast American actor Broderick Crawford in the role of an aging swindler in *Il bidone (The swindle)*. Based partly on stories told to him by a petty thief during production of *La strada*, Fellini developed the script into a con man's slow descent to a solitary death, killed by his gang. Savaged by critics at the 16th Venice Film Festival, the film did miserably at the box office and was not distributed internationally until 1964.

While preparing *Nights of Cabiria*, a sad story of a prostitute, in the spring of 1956, Fellini learned of his father's death from cardiac arrest at the age of 62. Starring his wife Giulietta Masina, the film took its inspiration from news reports about a woman's decapitated head retrieved in a lake and stories by

Wanda, a shantytown prostitute Fellini had met on the set of *Il bidone*. The movie won an Academy Award as Best Foreign Film and earned his wife, Guilietta Masina, the Best Actress Award at Cannes for her performance. However it was *La dolce vita* which broke all box office records. Despite scalpers selling expensive tickets, crowds stood in line for hours to see an "immoral movie" before the censors banned it. In May 1960 the jury of the 13th Cannes Film Festival, presided over by Georges Simenon, unanimously awarded the Palme D'Or to the movie. In 1962, it received Oscar nominations for best director, screenplay, best art and set direction and best costumes in a black-and-white film. *La dolce vita* first coined the term *paparazzi*, derived from Paparazzo, journalist Marcello Rubini's (Marcello Mastroianni) photographer friend.

During the sixties, after his Italian neo-realism period (1950-1959), Fellini discovered the works of Carl Jung. After meeting Jungian psychoanalyst Dr. Ernst Bernhard, the founder of the analytical school in Italy, in early 1960, he read Jung's autobiography, *Memories, Dreams, Reflections*. Bernhard also recommended that Fellini consult the *I Ching* and keep a record of his dreams. What Fellini had initially accepted as "his extrasensory perceptions" and hypnagogic experiences such as his sense of physical vibrations, were now interpreted and warmly accepted and encouraged as psychic manifestations of the unconscious. Bernhard's focus on Jungian depth psychology proved to be the single greatest influence on Fellini's mature style and marked the turning point in his work from neo-realism to filmmaking that became more grotesque, surrealist and dream-like. Jung's seminal ideas on the *anima* and the *animus*, the role of archetypes and the collective unconscious directly influenced such films as *8½* (1963), *Juliet of the Spirits* (1965), *Satyricon* (1969), *Casanova* (1976), and *City of women* (1980).

It was Jung Romantic genius, that allowed people to understand that humans, himself included, could be at the same time western, modern, secular, civilized and sane, but also primitive, archaic, mythical and mad (Douglas, 1997, p. 21). Jung, like Fellini, was fascinated with studies of possession, multiple personality, seers, mediums, and trancers, as well with shamans, magnetizers and hypnotic healers (p. 27).

The *Book of Dreams* (Fellini, 2008), [1] which covers a period of 16 years of Fellini's life, was triggered and influenced by his attraction to psychology in

1 In this book I referred to either the original Italian version of the Book of Dreams or the English translation. Both were published almost simultaneously by Rizzoli. I quote the English version except where the Italian contains specific uses of language, including Fellinian jargon that are crucial to an understanding of the dream.

general and Jungian theory in particular. The book is a collection of this intimate and mostly unpublished material as reported under the encouragement and the guidance of Dr. Bernhard. This book was kept (but not completely concealed) in a drawer in his desk at his office. The first section, well written and organized, has 245 pages and goes from 1960 to 1968. The second section, more paratactic and dispersed, is 154 pages long and goes from 1973 to 1982.

As pointed out by Kezich (2008), this *Book* may be approached in various ways. From a historical, biographical standpoint it may be used as a source of subjective social and political commentary on this period (see also O'Grady, 2008). On the other hand, on a more intimate and introspective level, the *Book* is a source of hitherto unpublished information regarding the director's life and the processes and changes occurring in his inner world during this time. Therefore this *Opera* can be analyzed in a psychological and autobiographical way, as first-hand revelations and secrets disclosed to a general readership many years later. The book is an invitation to explore a mystery, an immense treasure trove, surreal hypotheses, unattainable fantasies and precognitions. There are clear similarities between his dreams and his filmography, as though his inner world and his creativity were involved in a constant, rich dialogue.

Exploiting *La dolce vita*'s success, financier Angelo Rizzoli set up Federiz, an independent film company in 1960 for Fellini and production manager Clemente Fracassi to discover and produce new talent. Condemned as a "public sinner", censored by the moral right for "indecency" and by the left for "decadence" for his *La dolce vita*, Fellini responded with *The temptations of Doctor Antonio*, part of the omnibus *Boccaccio '70*. His first color film, it was the sole project that was given the green light by Federiz. Infused with the surrealistic satire that characterized the young Fellini's work at *Marc'Aurelio*, the film ridiculed a moral crusader who goes insane trying to censor a billboard showing the gorgeous Valkyrie Anita Ekberg (the same actress in *La dolce vita*), espousing the virtues of milk (and her breasts).

The shooting of *Otto e mezzo* (*8½*) began on May 9, 1962. This movie was chaotic, with incessant improvisations on set, and had no apparent rationale. Fellini commented that he hoped to convey the three levels "on which our minds live: the past, the present, and the conditional - the realm of fantasy". After shooting finished on October 14, Nino Rota composed various circus marches and fanfares that would later become the signature tunes of the maestro's cinema. Nominated for four Oscars, *8½* won awards for best foreign language film and best costume design in black-and-white.

During the sixties, Fellini became increasingly attracted to parapsychology, and met Gustavo Rol, a former banker who introduced him to the world of extra-sensory perception and séances. In 1964, Fellini experimented with LSD-25 under the supervision of Emilio Servadio, his psychoanalyst during production of *La strada*. For years he was silent about what actually occurred that day, but he admitted in 1992 that "objects and their functions no longer had any significance". He apparently remembered little of what happened. He learned he had spoken for hours on end while pacing continuously around the room. Fellini interpreted his experience as "a flight, the impossibility of standing still – that my natural condition is to be in motion, on the move" (cited by Alpert, 1986, p. 179), a quality, typical of the god Hermes and Fellini the man.

In 1969, his *Satyricon,* a loose adaptation of the original Latin work by Petronius, was released. In March filming started on *I clowns* broadcast as a TV premier in December. In 1971 filming started on *Roma*. The following year *Fellini's Casanova,* loosely inspired by the history and the personal life of Casanova, won the Oscar for Best Costumes. Fellini received a lifetime achievement award at the 27th Cannes Film Festival in 1974. *Amarcord,* a semi-autobiographical coming-of-age comedy, won the Oscar for Best Foreign Language Film in 1975. In 1977 Fellini works on *La città delle donne (City of women)*, released in March 1980, which caused an uproar in feminist movements. In this dream-sequence film, Fellini expounds at length on the nature, complexities, attitudes, and issues of women and how this all relates to men who are "hunting" for sexual conquests.

One year later, he started filming *Prova d'orchestra (Orchestra rehearsal)*, which was released in February 1979. In April 1979 Nino Rota, the author of most of his music tracks, died in Rome. Rota was the musician who perfectly understood Fellini's aesthetics of cheer and melancholy, and was "able to read his friend's soul and translate his capricious mood swings into music" (Kezich, 2006, p. 126).

In October 1983 *E la nave va* (*And the ship sails on*) was released. The ship becomes a mirror of Western society, grown frivolous with too much comfort, immersed in solipsistic ritual, and preoccupied with everything that lies outside this world of privilege. On September 6, 1985 Fellini was awarded the Golden Lion for lifetime achievement at the 42nd Venice Film Festival. That same year, he became the first non-American to receive the Film Society of Lincoln Center's annual award for cinematic achievement. Despite his opposition to commercials, that year he made a one-minute ad for Barilla pasta entitled *High society- Rigatoni* (containing a vulgar sexual message since Rigatone, a pasta shape, means oral sex in Rimini slang).

Long fascinated by Carlos Castaneda's *The Teachings of Don Juan*, Fellini accompanied the Latino-American author on a journey to the Yucatán to assess the feasibility of a film, which was never made.

In 1986, *Ginger and Fred,* a pathetic story of two aged dancers was released, and opened in February at the 36th Berlin Film Festival. In March, in New York with Giulietta at the premiere, he accepted a medal for lifetime achievement from Elia Kazan.

For *Intervista*, produced by Ibrahim Moussa and RAI Television, Fellini interspersed memories of the first time he visited Cinecittà in 1939 with present-day footage of himself at work on a screen adaptation of Franz Kafka's *Amerika.* A meditation on the nature of memory and film production, where the director directs himself as the actor, the film won the special 40th Anniversary Prize at Cannes and the 15th Moscow Film Festival Grand Prize. In Brussels later that year, a panel of thirty professionals from eighteen European countries named Fellini the world's best director and *8½* the best European film of all time.

In February 1989 Fellini took part in demonstrations against commercials during the televised broadcasts of movies. In early 1989, began production on his last film, *The voice of the moon.* Despite its modest critical and commercial success in Italy, and its warm reception by French critics, it failed to interest North American distributors.

In July 1991 and April 1992, Fellini worked in close collaboration with Canadian filmmaker Damian Pettigrew to establish "the longest and most detailed conversations ever recorded on film". Passages from this conversation in French are reported in this book. Described as the "Maestro's spiritual testament" by his biographer Tullio Kezich, excerpts culled from these conversations later served as the basis of their feature documentary, *Fellini: I'm a Big Liar* (2002) and the book, *I'm a Born Liar: A Fellini Lexicon.* In April 1993, Fellini received his fifth Oscar for lifetime achievement "in recognition of his cinematic accomplishments that have thrilled and entertained audiences worldwide".

Despite his opposition to commercials, in June 1992 he again started working on three new commercials for *Banca di Roma.* In March 1993 he received the Lifetime Achievement Award at the Oscar ceremony in Los Angeles. On June 28, he underwent heart bypass surgery. Partially paralyzed, he was first transferred to Ferrara for rehabilitation and then to Rome to be near his wife, also hospitalized. He suffered a second stroke and fell into an irreversible coma. Four days before his death, Martin Scorsese inaugurated an eight-week tribute *Tutto Fellini* at the Film Forum in New York. Fellini died in

Rome on October 31 at the age of 73, a day after his fiftieth wedding anniversary. The memorial service was held in Studio 5 at Cinecittà and was attended by an estimated 70,000 people. Five months later on March 23, 1994, Giulietta Masina died of lung cancer. Fellini, Masina and their son are buried in a bronze sepulcher in Rimini. The Federico Fellini Airport in Rimini is named in his honor.

FILMS DIRECTED BY FELLINI

In all his movies Fellini dealt with the relationship between illusion and reality, thus leading to the episodic and structural weaknesses of his films. His intention was to create fixed types, symbols, rather than more complex, psychologically evolving plots and figures (Baranski, 1993, p. 70), with their own traditional characters, descriptive precision, historical fidelity or elegant narrative construction (Fellini quoted in Markulin, 1993, p. 140).

Fellini's movies in general can be seen as baroque filigree opera. His movies lacked linearity and were embedded with metaphorical messages from the very beginning. According to Marcus (1993, p. 96), *La strada* clearly showed that his filmmaking would not confine itself to the material conditions of life, in a given time or place, according to the orthodox neorealist canon, but would transcend such limits to embrace metaphysical reality, spiritual reality and objective/ subjective attitudes.

As stressed in this book, Fellini's movies are always in a state of liminality. They are dreamlike, vague, ambiguous, and have no clear plot or center. The flow is more paratactic, associative, incidental, circumstantial and circular. What they lose in permanent structure they gain in continuous movement. As Foreman suggested, Fellini's pattern is to abandon "its chronological progression to find a more circuitous route to the center" (Foreman, 1993, p. 163). Like dreams, the episodes are mostly detached from each other. Situations and pictures reappear in a different guise in other movies, like in repetitive dreams; for example the theme of frescos appears in *Satyricon* and also in *Roma*, the figure of the prostitute Cabiria is found in *White sheik* and *Le notti di Cabiria*. For many reasons the characters of his films are like *Il viaggio di G. Mastorna* the movie, he never made:

> It becomes like an imagined, a dreamt journey, a journey in memory, in repressed knowledge, in a labyrinth with an infinity of exits, but only one entrance, and therefore the only problem is not going out but going in

> to it, and [if] I shamelessly would continue to pour out definitions and proverbs, I am not sure that I could suggest the sense of the movie, which I first and foremost don't know what it is. (Fellini quoted in Secchiaroli, 2000, p. 13).

FILMOGRAPHY

Luci Del Varietà (Variety Lights) (1950) (Co-Credited with Alberto Lattuada)

The film tells a story about people living in their tawdry world of one-night stands in dreary theaters, who somehow manage to surmount failure and hang on to their illusions of ultimate triumph. Battered by the hard facts of their existence, they maintain a touching faith (Alpert, 1988, p. 72), and commitment to their profession. A scrappy, aged, small-time actor, interpreted by De Filippo, becomes Pygmalion to a young girl, falls in love with her, helps her become an actress, and then loses her, when she start a better and promising new career. Bondanella (1992, p.79) argued that *Luci del varietà* revealed a "structural pattern inherent in the film's simple plot – the inevitable clash of dreams or illusions with a much harsher reality" a pattern which would be found also in the *White sheik* and *I vitelloni*.

Lo Sceicco Bianco (The White Sheik) (1952)

Ivan is in Rome on his honeymoon. Wanda, his bride, soon disappears from the hotel. Wanda sneaks away to the editorial offices of the weekly graphic magazine *Blue Enchantment*, wanting to meet the hero of her dreams, Fernando Rivoli, aka the White Sheik. She wrote many letters to, signing them "the passionate doll". In a trancelike state, Wanda boards a truck and follows the crew to Fregene where they are going to shoot an adventure sequence on the water. The young bride is captivated by this new world, which is actually revealed here in all its grotesque squalor. Meanwhile, Ivan is scouring Rome for her. The newlyweds are reunited in the end, after narrowly averting tragedy, and wind up in Saint Peter's Square, waiting to be received by the Pope along with 200 other couples.

I Vitelloni (The Vitelloni or Young and Passionate) (1953)

Vitelloni comes from *vidlon*, a dialectal term in Rimini slang that working people use to refer to students and bourgeois young men living in towns along the Adriatic coast and the idle frittering their way through steamy summers and the long days of winter. The vanity and inflated characters evoked in the movie wear outsize coats, fedoras, long scarves and have small mustaches. The movie is divided into four main parts. The first section is an account of the shotgun wedding between Fausto and pregnant Sandra, Moraldo's sister. The second episode takes place while they are away on their honeymoon, and depicts the boring everyday life of the loafer *vitelloni*. In the third episode, we watch Fausto fail in a halfhearted attempt to hold down a steady job in a religious artifacts store: he tries to seduce the owner's wife and is fired. In the last episode, a variety show comes to town. Fausto once again betrays his wife with a lovely soubrette. His behavior results in an unprecedented marital crisis, which with difficulty is nonetheless resolved. After the couple reconciles and heads home the narrator explains: "The story of Leopoldo, Alberto, Riccardo, and the rest of us… well you can imagine how it goes". The only one who escapes this fate is Moraldo, who, like Fellini years before, leaves on a personal quest to the big city.

Un'agenzia Matrimoniale (A Matrimonial Agency) (Segment from L'amore in Città- Love in the City) (1953)

The story follows a fearless journalist into the bowels of a huge building in Rome as he looks for the marriage agency Cibele. The journalist tells the agency owner that he has a childhood friend who lives in the country with his wealthy parents. He says that doctors think marriage may be his friend's only hope. A few days later the woman finds a candidate for him, Rossana, whom she presents to the journalist, sending the girl off with the admonition: "Do you understand, you are going to be a lady?". The journalist tells her that her date is a very rich man who suffers from lycanthropy – the moon has a terrible effect on him. The girl is entirely sympathetic. For her, a poor girl, marrying a wolf-man has advantages: "if he is nice, I know myself, I can grow attached". The journalist isn't prepared for such an honest sincere answer and does not have the courage to continue his ploy. At this point the movie abruptly ends.

La Strada (The Road) (1954)

This movie is considered the climax of Fellini's cinematic realistic period. It can be seen as a new perspective on Italian reality in that it depicts the impoverished country, the cold muddy fields, the primitive, even brutal relations between men and women; the peasant world at the margins of reconstruction; lost languages' magic and childhood (Kezich, 2006, p. xiv). Gelsomina a young woman, "not quite right in the head", is sold for 10,000 lire by her impoverished mother to, Zampanò, a gypsy to replace her deceased sister Rosa. Zampanò makes a living as an itinerant strongman, entertaining crowds by breaking an iron chain just by expanding his chest, and then passing around a hat for tips. He trains Gelsomina to play the snare drum and trumpet, dance a bit, and clown for the audience. Despite her willingness to please, he relies on intimidation and even cruelty at times to maintain his domination. Gelsomina is raped by Zampanò. Naïve and innocent to the point of foolishness, she is almost saint-like in her inchoate understanding of the suffering of others (Alpert, 1988, p. 94). Gelsomina meets *Il Matto*, the Fool, who persistently mocks Zampanò, and shows her that there are alternatives to her servitude. He talks her out of leaving Zampanò, imparting to her his philosophy that everything and everyone has a purpose, even a pebble, even her. She decides that hers is to take care of her unappreciative master. Over the course of his travels, Zampanò comes upon *Il Matto* fixing a flat tire on an empty stretch of road. He punches the clown several times and, satisfied with his revenge, starts to leave. *Il Matto* complains that his watch has been smashed, then unexpectedly collapses and dies. Zampanò hides the body and pushes his car off the road. Zampanò is relieved to escape unseen, but the killing breaks Gelsomina's spirit. After ten days, she is still unable to deal with her grief. When he cannot bear it any longer, he abandons her while she is taking a nap. Four or five years later, Zampanò is drawn to a woman singing a tune Gelsomina often played. He learns that the woman's father had found Gelsomina on the beach and kindly taken her in. Then she died. Zampanò gets drunk and wanders to the beach, where he breaks down and cries uncontrollably.

As far as Fellini's own itinerary is concerned, *La strada* can be seen as a distant prelude to *8½* with its abolition of any "hierarchy of realms", through a paratactic ordering of dreams, fantasy, memory and actuality. The journey of the actors, as vagrants, has no clear direction. For Stoddart:

> In *La strada* the dominant metaphor of the film seems to be 'the road of life' but that metaphor is complicated by all three of the circus players who dominate the film's drama...whose acts do not reflect the linear progression implied by the image of the road so much as an insistent circularity of movement, especially during performance. Their psychic development is fuelled by returns to familiar physical environments along what becomes a kind of circular road. (2002, p. 49)

Il Bidone (The Swindle and also the Swindlers) (1955)

Bidone is an Italian slang expression meaning scam, swindle, or slightly over-the-top deception or prank. The movie coincides with a calmer moment: Italian life is settling into reconstruction and on a path to economic growth, people need to rely less on scheming for their survival, but others must still preserve the art of living by wits alone. The plot follows various episodes of a gang of swindlers who prey upon peasants in the countryside. The film focuses on Augusto, the now aging leader of the gang. Some of these scenes include the gang attempting to extort money from the elderly, pulling a con scheme on helpless people, and so on. The film ends with the murder of Augusto, by his gang, when he attempts to swindle them.

Le Notti Di Cabiria (The Nights of Cabiria) (1957)

The film follows, Cabiria, a prostitute, as she searches for love and rehabilitation but encounters frequent heartbreak. Mistreated and taken advantage of by almost everybody she encounters, Cabiria eventually meets a man who promises her a respectable future and falls head over heels in love with him. His name is Oscar and he claims to be an accountant who is lonely too. Cabiria, suckered in with the hope of final redemption, sells her hovel of a house and withdraws her life savings from the bank to serve as a dowry. Taken to a lake by Oscar, Cabiria begins to realize that he is not all that he claims, and that he was a fake, and that once again she has been taken advantage of. She loses all her money, but manages to save her life.

La Dolce Vita (1960)

Seven episodes, mostly in Rome, linked by the journalist Marcello Rubini, make up this film that includes an evening with lovers, the adventures of an American movie star, an aristocratic party and an orgy. The theme is predominantly café society, the diverse and glittery world rebuilt upon the ruins and poverty of the postwar period, in the eternal and cosmopolitan metropolis. It is depicted as a kingdom for the few carefree people who flit from parties and cruises to scandals and follies. The film is a tragic allegory of the desolation lurking behind the façade of perpetual carnival. From one point of view the orgy corresponds to the pre-creation state of non-differentiation or a return to the cosmic night. The waters, in order to ensure complete regeneration of life and hence the fertility of the earth and an abundance of crops (Eliade, 1987, p. 147). Orgy can be seen in Fellini movies as a 'secret worship'. For scholars who analyzed this movie, the spiritual life of the protagonist covers just such a progression, but each step moves Marcello toward his spiritual death rather than salvation (Alpert, 1986, p. 147). Other writers have interpreted this movie as Dante's journey through the various circles of Hell, where Marcello observes and only passively participates in the various evils and perversion of modern life. The scale of evil extends downward from the natural sins of the flesh to the much more reprehensible perversions of intellect.

Le Tentazioni Del Dottor Antonio (The Temptations of Doctor Antonio) (Segment in Boccaccio '70) (1962)

Doctor Antonio Mazzuolo is a moralist. He is unmarried, and lives with his mother and sister. He finds lovers necking in cars and calls the cops on them. One day a billboard advertising milk, with a huge and provocative woman is put up facing his window. Shocked, Antonio crusades to have the billboard removed. He becomes obsessed by this image and goes insane. This short movie is a comment on Italian bigotry and the hypocrisy that condemned Fellini for *La dolce vita*.

Otto EeMezzo (8½) (1963)

This movie is considered Fellini last neo-realist film, and contains a great deal of auto-biographical themes. Guido Anselmi, a famous Italian film director, is suffering from writer's block. Artistic and marital difficulties cause him to lose interest. As Guido struggles half-heartedly to work on the film, a series of flashbacks and dreams reveal his memories and fantasies; they are frequently interwoven with reality. Guido's search for a kind of personal liberation is similar to Fellini's own "attempts to throw off the upbringing I have had; I try to uneducate myself by plunging again into the collective whole, so as not to remain subject to laws which are not my own, which are not anyone's because they are collective" (in Alpert, 1986, p. 177).

Giulietta Degli Spiriti (Juliet of the Spirits) (1965)

This is the portrait of an educated middle-aged woman. Giulietta, a bourgeois Gelsomina (also interpreted by Giulietta Masina), has learned how not to be a martyr, how to stand on her own two feet, how not to depend on her husband. This is her only way to banish the ghosts who persecute her, spirits that haunt the house and make themselves felt, like three dimensional dreams (Kezich, 2006, p. 259). Giulietta explores her subconscious and the odd lifestyle of her sexy neighbor, Suzy, as she attempts to deal with the mundane life and philandering husband who dominates her. As she increasingly taps into her desires, as well as her demons, she slowly gains more self-awareness and, ultimately, more independence.

Toby Dammit (Segment of Histoires Extraordinaires) (1968)

Former Shakespearean British actor Toby Dammit (a name which sounds like "to-be-damned") is ruining his acting career as he succumbs to alcohol. He agrees to work in Rome on a "Catholic-Western film" where his payment is also a Ferrari. The movie begins with the arrival of an airplane. The hero explains: "This is my first time to Rome and I have the feeling that this will be an important trip in my life". Under the influence of alcohol and drugs, the actor is fighting an enemy that only he can see as a hallucination: the devil in the form of a little girl who has lost her ball. Fellini thought that a man with a black cape and a beard was the wrong kind of devil for a drugged, hipped actor. His devil must be his own immaturity; hence, a white girl (discussed in Alpert, 1986, p. 197). Toby takes part in an absurd awards ceremony. He delivers a confused speech. After being awarded his Ferrari and while drunk, he speeds to the center of Rome. Workers try to get him to stop before the car goes across a collapsed bridge over a ravine, but he races ahead. When his car gets to the other side, his head has been severed by a wire that was stretched across the ravine. The young girl, the devil, is seen again, collecting his head.

Block-Notes Di Un Regista (A Director's Notebook) (1969)

In this semi-documentary film Fellini discusses his views on making motion pictures and his unorthodox procedures. He seeks inspiration in various out of the way places. During this film viewers go with him to the Coliseum at night, on a subway ride past Roman ruins, the Appian Way, a slaughterhouse, and on a visit to Marcello Mastroianni's house which is being ambushed by a busload of tourists. Fellini is also seen in his own office interviewing a series of unusual characters looking for work, holding auditions for his *Satyricon*. The audition sequence is both amusing and sad; it is a parade of pathetic, wistful types, all hoping to meet the master's specifications for parts in his new film (Alpert, 1988, p. 203).

This plot shows a pattern typical of Fellini filmography in that the workings of film making are part of the film itself: Fellini is the director and the subject of his movies when the technical movie team is transformed into actors as well (see also his *Intervista*).

Satyricon (Also Known as Fellini Satyricon) (1969)

Loosely based on the Petronius story, the movie describes the decadence of Imperial Rome in a surrealistic and fragmentary, paratactic fashion. There is no continuity, beginning or end. The film opens with Encolpio (Encolpius in the Latin original) lamenting the loss of his lover Gitone (Giton) to Ascilto (Ascyltus). Vowing to win him back, he learns at the Roman baths that Ascilto sold Gitone to the actor Vernacchio. Encolpio storms onto the stage and reclaims Gitone. Later they walk through the vast Roman brothel known as the Lupanare, observing numerous sensual scenes. At that moment, an earthquake destroys the building. Then Encolpio meets the poet Eumolpo (Eumolpus) at the art museum. The elderly poet blames the current corruption on the mania for money and invites his young friend to a banquet held at the villa of Trimalchione (also known as Trimalchio), a wealthy freeman. Captured by soldiers, Encolpio is released in a labyrinth and forced to play Theseus to a gladiator's Minotaur for the amusement of the spectators at the festival of the God of Laughter. When the gladiator spares Encolpio's life, the festival rewards the young man with Ariadne, a sensual woman with whom he must mate as the crowd looks on. Impotent, Encolpio is publicly humiliated by Ariadne. Encolpio and Ascilto hire a boatman to take them to Enotea's home (also known as Enothea). Greeted by an old woman who has him drink a potion, Encolpio falls under a spell where his sexual prowess is restored to him by Enotea (Enothea) in the form of an Earth Mother figure and sorceress. When Ascilto is murdered in a field by the boatman, Encolpio decides to join Eumolpo's ship bound for North Africa. But Eumolpo has died in the meantime, making his heirs all those willing to eat his corpse. "And here a new story begins" the voice of the narrator says.

Fellini allowed an American journalist and independent film maker Gideon Bachman to make his own documentary on the making of this film called *Ciao Federico!* (Alpert, 1986, p. 204), and again Fellini became an actor performing as a director.

I Clowns (The Clowns) (1970)

This is a film about Fellini's recurrent fascination with clowns and the circus. It was made for the Italian TV channel RAI with the stipulation that it would be released simultaneously on TV and as a cinema feature. Fellini reminisced about going to the circus as a child:

> I was as if struck by lightning: as if all of a sudden I had recognized something which had always belonged to me and was also my future, my work, my life. The clowns – who were weird, grotesque, shuffling along, and dressed in rags – seemed to me in their complete irrationality, their violence, and their abnormal capriciousness like drunken and delirious ambassadors of a vocation without escape, an anticipation, a prophecy: the *annunciation made to Federico*. And, in fact, the cinema – that is making films – living together with a crew that is shooting a film, isn't this like the life of the circus? (quoted in Risset, 1993, p. 65)

In fact, movies are pictures in perpetual motion, and like circus they escort us into a different reality. The film, one of Fellini's most appealing, turned out to be less a documentary than a personal film essay in three main parts. The first dealt with his recollection of circuses and clowns he had seen as a child; the second with a search for the clowns of old, their routines, and the meaning of their clownish acts; the third, as might have been expected, his own clown fantasia, an apotheosis of *clowndom* (Alpert, 1988, p. 223). In this film Fellini becomes an actor, performing the role of director and in many ways he becomes a clown himself.

Fellini Roma (1972)

Fellini repeatedly contrasts Roman life in wartime Fascist Italy with its counterpart in the early 1970s. The wartime scenes emphasize the neighbors who congregate in Rome's public places such as brothels, street restaurants, a variety show, and a bomb shelter. Fellini draws a parallel between the parade of prostitutes in wartime brothels and a fantasy runway fashion show featuring clerical garb and a papal audience. The plot centers on two journeys to Rome by the director. The first took place as a young man in the late 1930s or early 1940s. The second took place as the director of a film crew shooting a movie about Rome in the early seventies. The film alternates between these two narratives. *Roma* signals a shift in the structure of Fellini's films, in that the film is even more fragmentary, unhinged and intimate. Throughout his adventures in the city as a big metaphorical mother-whore, Fellini chatters freely, suspended between past and present (Kezich, 2006, p. 306). The final and most haunting scene in *Roma* occurs late at night. The city has grown silent. There is a sudden roar of motorcycles and a horde of cyclists erupts out of the darkness (Alpert, 1986, p. 235). Are these new Barbarians invading the Eternal City?

Amarcord (1973)

The movie depicts the Rimini of Federico's youth, and spans one spring season to the next in a "depressing Italian provincialism" (Kezich, 2006, p. 312). The structure of the film is based on small local anecdotes, memories (Amarcord means "I remember" in Romagna dialect), with a beginning and end following the seasons of the year, presented in a mocking tone, and always somehow modified by the fantastic and the absurd. A young woman hanging clothes on a line happily points out the arrival of "manine" or puffballs floating on the wind. In the village square, schoolboys jump around trying to pluck puffballs out of the air. Fellini presents his series of comic characters including a blind accordion player relentlessly tormented by schoolboys, Volpina, the stringy blond nymphomaniac, the stout and buxom tobacconist, Titta the rosy-cheeked adolescent protagonist based on one of Fellini's childhood friends, and Aurelio, Titta's father, a building contractor from a working-class background. Modest and reserved, Aurelio responds with frenzied anger to Titta's pranks while Miranda, his wife, always comes to her son's defense. In tow are Titta's grandfather, a likeable childish old goat with an eye on the family's young maid, and a street vendor, Biscein, the town's inveterate liar. Fascist parades and violent investigations and persecutions of dissidents (Titta's father included), adolescent sexual fantasies, pranks, marriages, dances , scenes from the classroom, a car race, are among fragments of these fantastic personal memories.

Il Casanova Di Federico Fellini (Fellini's Casanova) (1976)

A carnival in Venice is the prelude to a series of erotic encounters that follow Giacomo Casanova through the cities of 18th century Europe. Casanova's life, as subjectively interpreted by Fellini, becomes a freakish journey into sexual abandonment. Any meaningful emotion or sensuality is eclipsed by increasingly strange situations. In Venice, he "defiles" a fake nun for the pleasure of a rich voyeur; in Paris, he attempts to transfer a mature woman's soul into a man's through intercourse; in Dresden, his body is pounded by two hefty women and a hunchback. The narrative presents Casanova's adventures in an extravagant, detached and methodical fashion, as the respect he yearns for is constantly undermined by more basic urges. The script also highlights other incidents from the "real" Casanova's life, including his escape from a Venetian prison and his visit to a London Frost fair.

As Fellini stressed:

> I would have liked to get once and for all at the essence of cinema and the complete movie. Which means transforming the film into a painting, the goal would be to make a movie that is just a single shot, one image that would be eternally fixed and constantly rich with movements. (quoted in Kezich, 2006, p. 328)

Prova d'Orchestra (Orchestra Rehearsal) (1978)

This film was originally made for Italian TV, and later given limited release in the US. Using a symphony orchestra as a metaphor for mankind or the political situation in Italy, Fellini explores the various joys, sorrows, frustrations and triumphs of the musicians. The music heard throughout was written by *Nino Rota.* The film can be seen as an allegory, a reflection on the leftist youth movement of 1968 and its demise, viewed a decade later. It reflects on the disintegrating sense of personal responsibility and political anti-professionalism that were its consequences. In this movie there is a mixture of accents and idioms from different regions in Italy. Together the musicians are able to produce a musical performance that has a certain harmony, but in fact, their backgrounds and internal squabbles and constant pranks result in a total loss of discipline and self-control. The well ordered orchestra becomes a chaotic orgy. Only a last attempt to restore order by the German director of the orchestra puts the musician back in line.

La Città delle Donne (City of Women) (1980)

Snaporaz (*Marcello Mastroianni)* follows a woman off the train and through a field and then loses her. Soon, as a representative of the male sex in general he finds himself in a hotel, among myriad women attending a feminist conference. Surreal episodes take him through a villa with his alter-ego Dr. Katzone, and there are numerous references to his sexual exploits. Reunited with his former wife for a moment, he starts another sequence which reviews his past. At the end of the movie, we discover that this was just a dream. When responding to criticism from feminist activists in Italy, Fellini maintained his typical apolitical stance, saying this movie "doesn't have anything to do with feminism. A journey into femininity? What are you talking about? It is just buffoonery, a little variety show."

E La Nave Va (and the Ship Sails on) (1983)

A large ship in the middle of the ocean is a persistent symbol in Fellini's mythology (see for example the Rex in *Amarcord*). Crossing the ocean is a recurrent theme in his dreams. The ship, in this symbolism is both navel and naval: referring to a burial shrine likened to a ship and the mother's womb at the same time (Walker, 1983, p. 934). This time, a small boat pulls up alongside the liner and an enchanted visitor climbs aboard, traveling back in time to when the oceangoing cities were the mausoleums of good life (Kezich, 2006, p. 349). The film opens by depicting a scene in July 1914 immediately before the cruise ship *Gloria N.* set sail from the port of Naples. The opening sequence is in sepia tones, as though it were a period film, with no sound other than the whirring of the projector. Gradually the sepia fades into full color and we can hear the actors speaking.

Orlando, an Italian journalist, supplies commentary by directly addressing the camera, explaining to the viewer that the cruise is a funeral voyage to scatter the ashes of opera singer Edmea Tetua near the island of Erimo, her birthplace. Considered the greatest singer of all time, Tetua is celebrated for her goddess-like voice. The passengers include other opera singers, voice teachers, orchestra directors, theatre producers, actors, prime ministers, counts, princesses, and the stricken fans of the deceased diva. An awful stench rises from the ship's hold which turns out to be a love-sick rhinoceros neglected by the ship's crew. The beast is pulled up, washed on deck, and returned to the hold with fresh water and hay.

On the third day of the voyage, the passengers discover a crowd of shipwrecked Serbians camped on the deck of the ship. Fleeing in rafts towards Italy after the assassination at Sarajevo (which triggered the First World War), the refugees were brought on board the previous night by the captain. The Grand Duke and his men, however, are convinced the Serbians are terrorists and order the captain to confine the group to a corner of the ship. The upshot is a heady mix of cultures, both ethnic and artistic, where aristocrats and snobs joyfully share the stage (the ship's deck) with peasants and vibrant Serbian folklore.

But the revelry ends when the menacing flagship of the Austro-Hungarian fleet sails into view, demanding the return of the Serbian refugees. The captain agrees on condition that Edmea Tetua's ashes are scattered to the winds. After the ceremony, the refugees are loaded into a lifeboat for delivery to the Austrians but a young Serbian hurls a bomb at the flagship, causing pandemonium. The Austrians respond by cannon-fire. The *Gloria N.* sinks while aristocrats march to the lifeboats, a grand piano slides across the floor smashing mirrors, and butterflies twitter serenely above the melee of suitcases in the flooded corridors.

Ginger e Fred (Ginger and Fred) (1986)

The title is a reference to the American dancing couple Ginger Rogers and Fred Astaire. The two leads portray Italian impersonators of Astaire and Rogers who reunite after twenty years of retirement for a vulgar and bizarre television extravaganza featuring commercial channels. The movie is a complex and coherent indictment of the shallowness of commercial television, which, eager to squeeze commercials into every possible kind of program, deadens viewers' ability to appreciate complex or thought-provoking themes.

Fellini was critical of privately held networks, which developed in an anarchistic fashion in Italy toward the end of the 1970s. Obviously showing hundreds of movies for free each week on thousands of local stations drove an enormous number of viewers out of movie theaters; and it is understandable that a man of cinema like Fellini would be opposed to these channels. But what he finds most offensive are the insane commercial interruptions as they also appear in the movie (Kezich, 2006, p. 367).

Intervista (Interview) (1987)

This film was a television special, a typical blending of digression and intimacy whose beginnings can be traced back to 1968, with *A director's notebook*. Interviewed by a Japanese TV crew for a news report on his latest film, Fellini takes the viewer behind the scenes at Cinecittà. Fellini accompanies the Japanese TV crew on a brief tour of the studios. As they walk past absurd TV commercials in production, Fellini's casting director introduces him to four young actors that she has found to interpret Karl Rossmann, the leading role in the maestro's film version of Kafka's *Amerika.* Fellini describes the first time he visited Cinecittà as a journalist in 1938 during the Fascist era. Past and present intermingle as Fellini interacts with his younger self played by aspiring actor Sergio Rubini. Marcello Mastroianni appears in a TV commercial as Mandrake the Magician, and is taken on a visit to Anita Ekberg's house where she and Mastroianni re-live their *La dolce vita* scenes. Subject and object, fantasy and reality are intertwined.

La Voce della Luna (The Voice of the Moon) (1990)

With a nod to the lunar-obsessed lyrics of Italian poet Giacomo Leopardi, this acerbic tale focuses on the capture of the moon by the Micheluzzi Brothers while Ivo, newly released from a mental hospital, tries to seduce Aldina with whom he is infatuated. Although she wants nothing to do with him, Ivo equates her blond beauty with the moon, the origin of his madness and frustration. During his attempts to court her, he meets various madcap characters including an oboist who sleeps in the local cemetery, a man whose hobby is meditating on rooftops, and Gonnella, the ex-prefect fired for his rising paranoia. Gonnella makes Ivo his lieutenant and together they investigate the "wild conspiracies" around them.

Meanwhile, the three demented brothers have caught the moon using gigantic farming equipment and roped it down in a stable. What ought to be a sacred event becomes a squandered opportunity as priests, TV channels, and politicians turn it into a conference for official propaganda voiced to the assembled public. The conference rapidly degenerates into violence by a madman with a pistol screaming "What am I doing here? Why was I put here in the first place?" leaving Ivo to deliver the film's last words: "If we all quieted down a little, maybe we'd understand something."

FINALE

Hail to you (Hermes)
Son of Zeus and Maia.
I began this hymn
For you
And now I will pass on
To another hymn.
Farewell,
Dispenser of favors,
Guide,
Giver of good things.

Homer

ABOUT THE AUTHOR

Gabriel Cavaglion was born in Italy and immigrated to Israel in 1978. He is a social worker, a certified Jungian psychotherapist and Senior Lecturer in the School of Social Work and Department of Criminology at Ashkelon Academic College, Israel. He received his Ph.D. in Criminology from the Hebrew University of Jerusalem (1998). His research focuses on societal reaction to sects and cults in Israel, social construction of Satanism, ideologies of sexual education, and press coverage of filicide with particular emphasis on case studies in Israel in the last two decades. He has recently published academic papers on sex addiction and the internet, Satanism, the cultural glorification of crime (both of which appeared in *Folklore*), trafficking of women for sex, and a clinical case study published by the *Jungian Journal of Theory and Practice*.

REFERENCES

Affron, C. (1993). Order and the space for spectacle in Fellini's 81/2. In P. Bondanella and C. Degli-Esposito (eds.), *Perspectives on Federico Fellini*, pp. 119-129, New York: Macmillan.

Alpert, H. (1988). *Fellini: A life*. New York: Marlowe and Company.

Angelucci, G. (1993). An interview completely for watching. In P. Bondanella and C. Degli-Esposito (eds.), *Perspectives on Federico Fellini*, pp. 180-186, New York: Macmillan.

Bakhtin, M. (1965). *Rabelais and his world.* Cambridge: The M.I.T. Press.

Baranski, Z. (1993). Antithesis in Fellini's *I Vitelloni.* In P. Bondanella and C. Degli-Esposito (eds.), *Perspectives on Federico Fellini*, pp. 70-86, New York: Macmillan.

Bly, R. (1988). *A little book on the human shadow*. New York: Harper Collins.

Bondanella, P. (1992). *The Cinema of Federico Fellini*. Princeton: Princeton University Press.

Bonnigal, D. (2002). Fellini's Amarcord: variations on the libidinal limbo of adolescence. In F. Burke and M. Waller (eds.) *Federico Fellini: Contemporary Perspectives*, pp. 137-154, Toronto: University of Toronto Press.

Braun, V. and Wilkinson, S. (2001). Socio-cultural representations of the vagina. *Journal of Reproductive and Infant Psychology*, *19*, 17-32.

Brown, N. (1990). *Hermes the thief: the evolution of a myth.* Great Barrington, MA: Lindisfarne Press.

Burke, G. (1997). At home with Mamma. *Time* (Europe), 7th July, vo. 150, no. 1.

Burke, F. (2002). Federico Fellini: Realism/Representation/ Signification. In F. Burke and M. Waller (eds.) *Federico Fellini: Contemporary perspectives*, pp. 26-46, Toronto: University of Toronto Press.

Calvino, I. (1993). The autobiography of a spectator. In P. Bondanclla and C. Degli-Espositi, *Perspectives on Federico Fellini*, pp. 25-30, New York: Macmillan Publishing.

Campbell, J. (1968). *The hero with a thousand faces*. Princeton: Princeton University Press.

Carotenuto, A. (1994). *Jung e la cultura del XX secolo*. Milano: Bompiani.

Conti, I. (1972). Fellini's 8½: A Jungian analysis (parte seconda). *Ikon, 82-83*, 123-170.

Creed, B. (1993). *The Monstrous-Feminine: Film, feminism, psychoanalysis*. London: Routledge.

Douglas, C. (1997). The historical context of analytical psychology. In P. Young-Eisendrath and T. Dawson, *The Cambridge companion to Jung*, pp. 17-34, Cambridge University Press.

Eco, U. (1993). Thoth, Fellini, and the Pharaoh. In P. Bondanella and C. Degli-Espositi (eds.), *Perspectives on Federico Fellini*, pp. 293-294, New York: Macmillan.

Ehrenzweig, A. (1967). *The hidden order of art*. London: Weidenfeld and Nicolson.

Eliade, M. (1959-1987). *The sacred and the profane: The nature of religion*. Orlando, Florida: Harcourt Brace Jovanovich, Inc.

Fellini, F. (1976). *Fellini on Fellini*. London: Eyre Methuen.

Fellini, F. (1978). Casanova: an interview with Aldo Tassone. In Bondanella P. (ed.) *Federico Fellini: Essays in criticism*, pp. 27-35, New York: Oxford University Press.

Fellini, F. (2007). *Il libro dei sogni*. Edited by Tullio Kezich and Vittorio Boarini Milano: Rizzoli.

Fellini, F. (2008). *The book of dreams*. Edited by Tullio Kezich and Vittorio Boarini, New York: Rizzoli.

Ferenczi, S. (1989). *Thalassa: A theory of genitality*. London: H. Karnac Books.

Foreman, W. (1993). Fellini's cinematic city: *Roma* and the myth of foundation. In P. Bondanella and C. Degli-Espositi (eds.), *Perspectives on Federico Fellini*, pp. 151-165, New York: Macmillan.

Fredericksen, D. (2005). Jung/sign/symbol/film. In C. Hauke and I. Alister (eds.)

Jung and Film: Post-Jungian takes on the moving image, pp. 17-55, New York: Routledge.

Free, W. (1973). Fellini's *I Clowns* and the grotesque. *Journal of Modern Literature, 3*, 214-227.

Gaillard, C. (2009). Dire e non detto del sogno, in Gaillard, C. and Ravasi Bellocchio, L. (2009). *L'inconscio creatore: Attorno al libro dei sogni di Federico Fellini*, pp. 9-59, Bergamo (Italy): Moretti and Vitali.

Gaillard, C. and Ravasi Bellocchio, L. (2009). *L'inconscio creatore: Attorno al libro dei sogni di Federico Fellini.* Bergamo (Italy): Moretti and Vitali.

Gaudenzi, C. (2002). Memory, dialect, politics: linguistic strategies in Fellini's *Amarcord.* In F. Burke and M. Waller (Eds.) *Federico Fellini: Contemporary perspectives*, pp.155-168, Toronto: University of Toronto Press.

Geduld, C. (1978). Juliet of the Spirits: Guido's Anima. In P. Bondanella (Ed.), *Federico Fellini: Essays in criticism,* pp. 137-151, New York: Oxford University Press.

Gilmore, D. (2003). *Monsters, evil beings, mythical beasts, and all manners of imaginary terror*. Philadelphia: University of Pennsylvania Press.

Guirand, F. (1993). Greek Mythology. In *New Larousse Encyclopedia of Mythology*, pp. 85-167, Slovenia: Reed International Books Limited.

Harding, E. (1997). *The I and not-I: A study in development of consciousness.* Princeton, NJ: Princcton Univcrsity Press.

Harpham, G. (1982). *On the grotesque: strategies of contradiction in art and literature*. Princeton: Princeton University Press.

Hauke, C. (2005). Let's go back to finding out who we are: Men, *Unheimlich* and the returning home in the films of Steven Spielberg. In C. Hauke and I. Alister (eds.), *Jung and film: Post Jungian takes on the moving image*, pp. 151-174, Routledge.

Hillman, J. (2005). *Senex and Puer.* Putnam, Connecticut: Spring Publications.

Jung, C.G. (1957). *Symbols of transformation*. London: Routledge and Kegan Paul.

Jung, C.G. (1963). *Memories, dreams, reflection*. London: Collins, Routledge and K. Paul.

Jung, C.G. (1970). *Alchemical studies*. Princeton, NJ: Princeton University Press.

Jung, C. G. (1983). Approaching the unconscious. In C.G. Jung (Ed.) *Man and his symbols*, pp. 18-103. San Sebastian, Spain: Ferguson Publishing Company.

Jung, C. G. (2001). *Four archetypes.* London: Roudledge.

Jung, C. G. (2009). *The Red Book.* New York: Norton.

Kayser, W. (1963). *The grotesque in art and literature.* Indiana: Indiana University Press.

Kerenyi, K. (1990). *Hermes guide of souls: The mythologem of the masculine source of life.* Dallas: Spring Publications.

Kezich, T. (2006). *Federico Fellini: His life and work.* New York: Straus and Giroux.

Kezich, T. (2008). Somni Explanatio or in the realm where everything is possible. In Fellini, F. (author), *The Book of Dreams,* pp. 9-18, New York: Rizzoli.

Kuryluk, E. (1987). *Salome and Judas in the cave of sex.* Evanston, Illinois: Northwestern University Press.

Lopez-Pedraza, R. (2003). *Hermes and his children.* Einsiedeln, Switzerland: Daimon Verlag.

MacLeod, D. (2006). Italian Mammas making offers their sons can't refuse. *The Guardian*, 3rd February.

Marcus, M. (1993). La Strada: Transcending neo-realism. In P. Bondanella and C. Degli-Espositi (eds.), *Perspectives on Federico Fellini*, pp. 87-99, New York: Macmillan.

Markulin, J. (1993). Plot and the character in Fellini's *Casanova*: Beyond *Satyricon.* In P. Bondanella and C. Degli-Espositi (eds.), *Perspectives on Federico Fellini*, pp.139-150, New York: Macmillan.

Miller, W. (1997). *The anatomy of disgust.* Cambridge, MA: Harvard University Press.

Moore, R. and Gillette, D. (1990). *King, Warrior, Magician, Lover: Rediscovering the archetypes of the mature masculine.* San Francisco: Harper.

Netzer, R. (2008). *The magician, the fool and the empress.* Ben Shemen, Israel: Modan (in Hebrew).

Neumann, E. (1991). *The Great Mother: An analysis of the archetype.*
Princeton: Princeton University Press.

Neumann, E. (1994). *The fear of the feminine.* Princeton: Princeton University Press.

O'Grady, D. (2008). Federico Fellini: The Book of Dreams, *Los Angeles Times*, Book Review, 8th June.

O'Healy, A. (2002). Interviews with the vamp: Deconstructing femininity in Fellini's final films (Intervista, La voce della luna). In F. Burke and M. Waller (eds.) *Federico Fellini: Contemporary perspectives,* pp. 208-232, Toronto: University of Toronto Press.

Otto, W. (1955). *The Homeric Gods: the spiritual significance of Greek religion*. London: Random House.

Paglia, C. (1990). *Sexual Personae: Art and decadence from Nefertiti to Emily Dickinson*. New York: Random House.

Paris, G. (1990). *Pagan grace: Dionysos, Hermes and Goddess Memory in daily life*. Dallas, Texas: Spring.

Pasolini, P.P. (1993). The Catholic irrationalism of Fellini. In P. Bondanella and C. Degli-Espositi (eds.), *Perspectives on Federico Fellini*, pp. 101-109, New York: Macmillan.

Pettigrew, D. (1994). *Federico Fellini: je suis un grand menteur*. Paris: L'Arche.

Picchietti, V. (2002). When in Rome do as the Romans do? Federico Fellini's problematization of femininity (The White Sheik). In F. Burke and M. Waller (eds.) *Federico Fellini: Contemporary perspectives*, pp. 92-106, Toronto: University of Toronto Press.

Pinkola Estès, C. (1992). *Women who run with the wolves*. New York: Ballantine Books.

Ravasi Bellocchio, L. (2004). *Gli occhi d'oro: il cinema nella stanza dell'analisi* .Bergamo, Italy: Moretti and Vitali.

Ravasi Bellocchio, L. (2009). Fellini e il femminile. In Gaillard, C. and Ravasi Bellocchio, L., *L'inconscio creatore: Attorno al Libro dei Sogni di Federico Fellini*, pp. 63-113, Bergamo, Italy: Moretti and Vitali.

Risset, J. (1993). The White Sheik: The annunciation made to Federico. In P. Bondanella and C. Degli-Espositi (eds.), *Perspectives on Federico Fellini*, pp. 63-69, New York: Macmillan.

Rossi, P. and Lawton, B. (1978). Reality, fantasy and Fellini. In Bondanella, P. (ed.) *Federico Fellini: Essays in criticism*, pp. 254-261, New York: Oxford University Press.

Salman, S. (1997). The creative psyche: Jung's major contributions. In P. Young-Eisendrath and T. Dawson, *The Cambridge companion to Jung*, pp. 52-70, Cambridge University Press.

Samuels, A., Shorter, B. and Plaut, F. (2003). *A critical dictionary of Jungian analysis*. New York: Taylor and Francis Group.

Secchiaroli, T. (2000). *G. Mastorna opera incompiuta*. Palermo, Italy: Sellerio.

Shalit, E. (2008). *Enemy, cripple and beggar: Shadow in the Hero's path*. Fisher King Press.

Shinoda Bolen, J. (1989). *Gods in everyman*. New York: Harper and Row.

Stein, M. (1983). *In midlife: A Jungian perspective.* Dallas: Spring Publications.

Stevens, A. (2002). *Archetype revisited: An updated history of the Self.* London: Brunner-Routledge.

Stoddart, H. (2002). Subtle wasted traces: Fellini and the circus. In F. Burke and M. Waller (eds.). *Federico Fellini: Contemporary perspectives*, pp. 47-64, Toronto: University of Toronto Press.

Storr, A. (1982). *Jung*. London: Harper Collins.

Stubbs, J. (2006). *Federico Fellini as auteur: Seven aspects of his films.* Carbondale: Southern Illinois University.

Vannoy Adams, M. (1997). The archetypal school. In P. Young-Eisendrath and T. Dawson, *The Cambridge companion to Jung*, pp. 101-118, Cambridge University Press.

Van Watson, W. (2002). Fellini and Lacan: The hollow phallus, the male womb, and the rethinking of the umbilical. In F. Burke and M. Waller (eds.) *Federico Fellini: Contemporary perspectives,* pp. 65-91, Toronto: University of Toronto Press.

von Franz, M.L. (1983). The process of individuation. In C.G. Jung (Ed.), *Man and is symbols*, pp. 158-229. San Sebastian, Spain: Ferguson Publishing Company.

von Franz, M.L. (1999). *Archetypical dimensions of the Psyche.* Boston: Shambala.

von Franz, M.L. (2000). *The problem of Puer Aeternus.* Toronto: Inner City Books.

Walker, B. (1983). *The woman's encyclopedia of myths and secrets.* San Francisco, CA: Harper and Row.

Willeford, W. (1969). *The fool and his scepter: a study in clowns and jesters and their audience.* London: Edward Arnold Publishers.

Williams, D. (2005). " If you could see what I've seen with your eyes…"; Post-human psychology and *Blade Runner.* In C.Hauke and I. Alister (eds.) *Jung and Film: Post Jungian takes on the moving image*, pp. 110-128, New York: Routledge.

Yalom, M. (1998). *A history of the breast.* New York: Alfred Knopf.

Yeoman, A. (1998). *Now or Neverland: Peter Pan and the myth of eternal youth; a psychological perspective on a cultural icon.* Toronto: Inner City Books.

INDEX

D

E

F

Q

R

S

T

U

V

W

Y